A Mother's Tears for a Missing Son

A Challenging Spiritual Experience

Cuddy,

God Bless

Dolly

A MOTHER'S TEARS FOR A MISSING SON

A CHALLENGING SPIRITUAL EXPERIENCE

BY DOLLY HILLS

PUBLICATION CONSULTANTS
We Believe In The Power Of Authors

PO Box 221974 Anchorage, Alaska 99522-1974
books@publicationconsultants.com—www.publicationconsultants.com

ISBN 978-1-59433-745-1
eISBN: 978-1-59433-746-8
Library of Congress Catalog Card Number: 2017951732

Manufactured in the United States of America.

Dedication

I dedicate *A Mother's Tears for a Missing Son* to all parents who have lost children, especially through the pain of *disappearance*. I hope this story, in some small way, will give comfort to those who have had a similar experience. My thoughts and prayers will always go out to these families.

In memory of Rick Hills
6/4/68–2/26/04 Age 35

Introduction

I started writing *A Mother's Tears for a Missing Son* shortly after my son Rick disappeared, knowing intuitively that I had to do this for my own healing of grief. This type of self-therapy was very difficult most of the time. Such strong emotions were involved. At times, there were long lapses between writings. I finally realized that I had to make the distinction between *writing* the story and *being* the story. It was such an emotional project, and as I wrote I learned to stand outside of the experience instead of being involved in it.

I also wrote *A Mother's Tears for a Missing Son* as a legacy for the grandchildren that Rick gave me. They can always turn to this book for memories of their father.

Keep an open mind as you read *A Mother's Tears for a Missing Son*. The content is not the recounting of an every day story. It was written from the heart. The experience was uniquely mine – but of a nature that wants to be shared.

Though this is a true story, some names have been changed for respect of privacy.

Chapter One

The dreaded moment had come. The dreaded moment had come! I knew this moment in time would arrive. I had relived it so many times—with tears streaming down my face. It was usually when I was driving down the road alone, having quiet time to myself. I would reflect upon this, pray, and then cry. It hurt so much. I was trying to prepare myself so when the time came I would be as strong as I could be to handle something so devastating as losing a son. I didn't know under what circumstances this would happen, but I knew from the bottom of my heart it would one day occur. Often after participating in Holy Communion during church Mass, I reflected upon this while kneeling in meditation. Again the painful tears would flow. But, it was always in passing. I could put the sad thoughts away after a while and be on my way.

It was Friday, February 27, 2004. My husband, Tom, and I were traveling from Phoenix, Arizona to Anchorage, Alaska en route to our home in Soldotna. We had a layover in Seattle. It was about seven o'clock in the evening. As we were going down the ramp to depart from Seattle to Anchorage, my cell phone started ringing. I noticed the phone number was Heidi's.

Heidi had been my oldest son Rick's partner for the past twelve years. When Heidi met Rick she already had a two-year-old daughter, Mackenzie, whom we've always loved and considered as our very own granddaughter. Heidi and Rick then had Rosie, who was now eight years old, and Calvin, who was now five. Mackenzie, whom we always referred to as "Mack," was now thirteen.

I didn't answer the cell phone because feelings of dread came over me. I just told myself that I would wait to arrive in Anchorage before I returned the call, because it was an inconvenient time to talk. Really, I was just too scared to answer it because of the timing of the phone call and the fearful feeling that enveloped me. So I embarked on the plane and put it out of my mind. It was a three-hour plane ride to Anchorage and I didn't want to worry about it. I got out a book and started reading to defocus from the worrisome thoughts in the back of my mind.

When the plane landed in Anchorage and we were waiting to get off, I mentioned to Tom that I had to call Heidi back. He made the comment, "Rick is probably in jail," because Rick always seemed to be in some kind of tight fix. My response was, "No, Tom, that would be good news," suggesting that at least Rick would be alive and well.

Just as soon as Tom and I walked inside the Anchorage airport from the plane, I called Heidi. She immediately answered the phone and I responded saying that I was returning her phone call. Her voice was solemn as she said, "I don't know how to tell you this so I'll just spit it out. Rick's truck was found abandoned on the

Kenai Keys road in Sterling, and Rick has been reported missing." In a panic-stricken voice, I replied, "What do you mean, MISSING?!" I knew exactly what she meant and immediately knew in my heart that Rick was dead. I instantly became very emotional and had to hand the cell phone to Tom. I was in a daze and had a hard time finding the way out of the airport. As I was going down the escalator I saw my niece, Shannon, standing on the bottom floor and smiling, not knowing the shocking news we had just received. To me she was just a blur because of the tears streaming down my face. I heard her ask Tom what was wrong and he replied that we had just heard from Heidi that Rick was missing. I barely remember leaving the terminal to go to the curbside to be picked up by Shannon's older sister, Gloria. When I got into the vehicle I could hear Tom explaining the situation. He was saying what Heidi had relayed—that the State Troopers had had a plane going over the area where Rick was missing and that rescue dogs had been used in the search, but had found nothing. The weather didn't help the search —it had been lightly snowing. I couldn't quit quietly crying. I couldn't talk, nor did I want to.

Gloria drove us to her house where we had parked our vehicle for the duration of our trip. She fixed us some coffee for the road but I couldn't drink it. I was just too distraught.

Tom and I took off for our hometown of Soldotna, 150 miles south of Anchorage. As we neared Girdwood thirty minutes out of Anchorage, Tom stopped off at the State Troopers station to see if he could get any updated information on Rick, but there weren't any new reports.

It was a long, dismal, and frustrating drive back to Soldotna. Because it was nighttime and snowing, it seemed even more taxing since we had to drive more slowly than normal. I told Tom at one point, as I grasped his hand, that I just didn't know how we were going to get through this! How can I explain the emotional pain I was feeling? Unbearable pain for one. And what was I thinking? I *couldn't* think! I know at times I was praying very hard to God to find Rick, though deep down I dreaded the worst. I really do believe a mother has true instincts, especially when it comes to her children. It was flashing through my mind that I had read or heard somewhere that it takes about two years for someone to go through a grieving process. I just couldn't imagine that, because the suffering of just the last few hours was intolerable. The news concerning Rick was so devastating. I was totally in shock and didn't realize it. Unbeknownst to me, I would be going through this process for the next two and half years.

Chapter Two

It was going on 10:30 p.m. that Friday evening as Tom and I drove into Soldotna. We went straight to Heidi's house. At this time I wasn't crying but remember being totally numb. Heidi explained how the State Troopers had come to her home late the night before to inform her that Rick's truck had been found left running and out of gas in the "Kenai Keys" area located near the Kenai River in Sterling, a small town ten miles north of Soldotna. A neighbor from that area had seen Rick's truck in the ditch around noon, and the truck had been running with the passenger door left open. Later that evening around five he noticed the truck was still there, but not running because it was now out of gas. It was also reported later that the truck was noticed by a newspaper delivery boy passing by around 4 a.m. that Wednesday. When Larry, a State Trooper, was notified of the situation, he drove out to the area to investigate. When he got there it was getting dark, so he proceeded to follow Rick's tracks with a flashlight in hand. It appeared that after getting out of the passenger side of the truck (the driver's side was up against a snowbank) Rick had crossed the road and started walking down a power line trail. Larry noticed as he followed Rick's tracks that his right leg was dragging. The officer proceeded down the power line trail, which wove in and out of a subdivision, and it looked like Rick wasn't sure where he was heading. He'd got off the trail at one point to walk up to an uninhabited cabin. It looked like he had tried to open the door, but it was locked. He left the porch and proceeded to get back on the power line trail and walked until he reached, "Feuding Lane Road" and then walked across the highway onto a road that led down to a small airstrip. A local tracking dog had been brought in, but Rick's tracks were lost because it had snowed a couple of inches that day. The tracking couldn't be continued until the next day, when a search and rescue team came with avalanche dogs. Rick's tracks were then picked up on the airstrip. They showed that he had walked up to and entered a private airplane hangar. He then left the hangar and walked back to the airstrip; thereafter it appeared his tracks disappeared into thin air!

Chapter Three

As Heidi continued, she reiterated that Rick had come back from his North Slope job the week before. On Tuesday, February 24, he had stopped by her workplace and said that he needed to drive to Anchorage to pick up his paycheck. He had seemed a little down and said that he really didn't want to go. She had encouraged him in a positive manner to just go and get the check and come back. They ended up laughing a little and he took off. That was the last time Heidi had seen or heard from Rick.

I found myself thinking about the last time Tom and I had seen Rick. It was right before we left on our trip on February 16. Rick had come over to the house and was talking to Tom in the garage. He was going to the North Slope and was looking for some work boots. I saw him very briefly. What really stood out in my mind was that a few days earlier, Heidi, Rick, Tom and I were playing cards and having an enjoyable evening. We had been getting together lately because Heidi had always wanted to learn to play pinochle. Tom and I had been playing for years. Rick was my partner because he always got along better with me than with Tom. Tom was Heidi's experienced partner.

I remember sitting directly across the table looking at Rick and distinctly hearing a voice in my head that said, "Enjoy him now because he won't be here for long." It was like a very quiet and clear message from Spirit. I felt very sad and helpless because I knew that I had no control over his destiny. I was solemn and didn't say anything to anybody because it was like a personal message. Internally I could feel that dreaded feeling concerning Rick (as I always did) because of his lifestyle. There was a dull pain in my heart but I just kept on talking and laughing on the outside to cover it up. I heard Heidi giggling and having a good old time because she was learning to "bid," which is really the trick to playing pinochle. I loved Heidi's laugh and it made me feel so much better.

As I quickly dismissed these comforting reminiscences, my thoughts came back to the present time. I had sensed what was going through Heidi's head that evening while we were at her house. I was thinking the same thing. We both knew that Rick always called home or made contact no matter what was going on in his life at the time. I recalled, in hindsight, that I had taught my two sons to always call home and check in out of courtesy to their loved ones. It was a request respected at all times. Because of this, Heidi and I knew deep down that something terrible had happened to Rick, and it was frustrating because at this point there were no answers.

With very heavy hearts, Tom and I left Heidi's house to go to our own home. We lived about six miles from town. As we were driving down our subdivision road

I looked at the snow berms and thought of how deep the snow still was and how it would be getting deeper because of the continuing snowfall. This would make things worse for finding signs in the search for Rick.

We got home and got ready for bed. It was late and we were very tired from our trip and from dealing with the devastating news. I felt so overwhelmed. But how in the world can anybody really sleep when no matter how tired you are, you have to process this kind of shock? You don't. You just doze off from exhaustion. Sleep comes in bits and pieces during the night. From that night on, to just keep my sanity, whenever I woke up during the night (which was many times), I would say either the Hail Mary or the Lord's Prayer over and over again until I fell back to sleep. I used this as a survival tool so I wouldn't allow myself to imagine the many horrible things that could have happened to Rick. I felt that God was, and would be, my only saving grace.

Chapter Four

B y the next day we started getting phone calls from friends and relatives. Along with the newspaper and the evening news reports, word of mouth traveled fast. I was too distraught to talk to anyone, and had to have Tom take all the phone calls. Because of this, several of my close friends got hurt feelings, not understanding that I *couldn't* talk to them. I explained to them a long time later that it wasn't that I didn't want to talk with them—it was just that every time I tried to talk I got a big lump in my throat and it felt like my voice box wouldn't work. I have always been like this whenever I was extremely upset emotionally.

Once in a while I was able to take a phone call if I happened to be in a stable space at the moment. One of those phone calls was from a friend of Rick's calling from Anchorage. It was only a couple of days after we had gotten back from our trip. John had been one of the last persons in Rick's company before he (Rick) drove to Soldotna. John strongly suggested that I hire a private investigator regarding Rick's disappearance. He did not go into any detail as to the reason why, but I could read between the lines. Since Rick had been involved in the drug world, his disappearance would be suspicious. People could have been after him for whatever reason. Now I got the feeling that perhaps foul play was involved, but I really didn't want to believe that at the time. It was enough to handle the fact that my son was missing, let alone thinking that it involved someone hurting him.

Heidi had contacted my brother Archie, and his fiancée, Clare, who lived in Palmer, Alaska. Clare worked at her family-owned business, Hartley Motors. They knew Rick well and were close to him. Clare immediately organized a group of snowmachiners from her business to come down to Soldotna to search for Rick in the area where he was reported missing. They transported about six snowmachines down and stayed at a local lodge, free of charge, because of the situation involved. My brother Archie was in the group, along with his son, Brian, and Clare's son, Grant. Rick was good friends with both boys. Other local friends and relatives who had snowmachines joined the group in the search. Some friends drove their vehicles looking around the area. This was the first week of March and the snow was still very deep and at times it was still snowing. This was a terrain that was riddled with snowmachine trails. They were looking for any tracks that led off a trail, which would be visible because the snow was waist-deep. It didn't look like you could travel very far because of the depth of the snow. My husband, Tom, told me later that he had gone over the area several times on snowshoes—a very large area of typical Alaskan wilderness terrain. Tom contacted a friend who owned an airplane so they could fly over the area and search also by air. It was like looking for a needle in a haystack. But we had to try every possible avenue.

I was so distraught that I was like a walking zombie. I couldn't even begin to think about going out to the area. I was too emotional and I couldn't think straight. I even dreaded going over to Heidi's house because it was unbearable to even see Rick's truck, which by now was in her driveway. *Everything* was painful that was related to Rick. It was even very difficult for me to walk into their home. Everything reminded me of him. Believe it or not, it was even hard for me to be around Rick's kids. It hurt so much because I could feel their pain and confusion.

The snowmachiners searched for two days, but did not find anything. They covered many, many miles and Tom and I were very grateful for their efforts. You could tell that my brother Archie was sadly disappointed that they didn't find anything. He told me that they tried very hard and apologized because it turned out to be futile. In spite of the disappointment, Archie could make me laugh, even in a sad situation like this. Everyone in our family has a huge sense of humor. Somehow we are always able to crack a few jokes. Even when crying on the inside, laughing on the outside made us feel better.

So, Archie and his group headed back to Palmer after a futile snowmachine search. I felt a sense of disappointment, but the search for Rick was to continue for a long time.

Chapter Five

After we were back for a few days, from our Phoenix trip, I contacted an acquaintance of mine who had a relative that was an intuitive and had worked with the Anchorage Police Department in investigations such as this.

Her name was Joan and I contacted her immediately when I got her Anchorage phone number and explained the situation. She agreed to meet with us. Tom and I made an appointment with her for the following day. She told us to bring a couple of pieces of Rick's clothing. I brought a shirt and a cap. We drove up to Anchorage and met her in her office in the early afternoon. Joan took the clothing in her hand and held them for a while and then took out a piece of paper with pen and started talking and drawing at the same time. She said that Rick was running (as in being chased) and that he was dragging his right leg because it had been injured after his truck ended up in the ditch. This information impressed Tom because he had not told any of this to Joan. The police had said the same thing after following Rick's tracks. Joan drew a detailed picture of a cabin with trees around it and a burn barrel in front. If Rick was running away from something, this information would make sense. After all, the truck was left running and his wallet with money was left in the front seat. Joan also drew something that looked like railroad tracks above the cabin on the picture. The cabin with the burn barrel that she drew was like a duplicate of the one that the police said Rick had walked up to and had tried to enter, but couldn't because the door was locked. This was information that we also had not disclosed to Joan. Tom figured later that the railroad tracks represented the telephone lines that you could see behind the cabin. Rick had followed a telephone line trail after leaving his truck.

Joan also drew a picture of the airstrip. She said that when Rick left the airplane hangar and walked to the airstrip a few yards away, a snowmachiner who had driven from the north end, a wooded area, picked him up. Joan also stated that Rick recognized the snowmachiner and had felt safe with this person. She said that they drove toward the south end of the airstrip toward the road. Joan said that she could only see the back side of the snowmachiner and that he or she had long blonde hair. She felt she would instantly recognize the person if she saw him or her directly.

It was only natural that after hearing this information, a loved one would feel some hope that Rick was still alive and safe. I wanted to believe this, but what kept going through my thoughts was that if Rick wasn't in his right mind because of drugs and couldn't think rationally, how in the world could he even use his survival skills to stay alive if the snowmachiner dropped him off someplace? This was all taking place on an early

February morning in Alaska, which was cold. I knew Rick was not dressed in warm enough clothing to be wandering around in this type of weather.

Fearful thoughts came to mind that maybe he got into a fight with somebody and was harmed or impaired so that he couldn't seek help.

You just can't imagine what goes through a mother's mind in this kind of situation—if Rick was still alive, was he in danger or pain? Was he not able to get to a phone because of physical impairment? Was he being held somewhere against his will? All of these extremely painful questions kept popping up in my mind. All I could do to keep from feeling like I was going insane was to pray constantly and I mean *constantly*!

Chapter Six

Now, going back in time, I realized that because I was in so much shock I couldn't get personally involved in searching the area where Rick went missing or even go near it. I also couldn't bring myself to go to the State Troopers' office to inquire or discuss the investigation at the time. Heidi, my younger son, Troy, and Kurt, who was a good friend of both my sons Rick and Troy, all went down to the State Troopers' office to discuss the situation with Larry. Larry was the State Trooper who had done the initial investigation by following Rick's tracks in the snow. Also, Kurt had been one of the last people to see Rick before he took off to Anchorage. So, hopefully, Kurt would be able to relay any kind of information that would be helpful in solving this mystery. Heidi, Troy, and Kurt were asked all kinds of questions such as: did Rick have any enemies that they were aware of, or was there anybody who would harm him for any reason? Who were his friends in Soldotna and Anchorage? Was he employed and where? Where did he hang out and with whom? What was his lifestyle? Now all four people knew Rick very well and knew that he was a partier. Larry had stated that they had found opened cans of beer in his truck and other paraphernalia that could indicate his thinking could have been impaired at the time.

At one point after this questioning, it hit Troy that something very serious could have happened to Rick and he could be dead. Troy became teary eyed and left the room.

I believe that he had been in denial up to this point and now realized his brother could be gone. It so happened that at the time when Rick disappeared, Troy and his wife, Peggy, were in Seattle for the weekend. Heidi had phoned Peg's mother, Debbie, to try and contact them about Rick's disappearance. Peggy told me later that she had tried to get an earlier flight home but couldn't. I always got the feeling that when Troy heard the news he put it in the back of his mind knowing that Rick was always getting in some sort of pinch, and that he'd probably just show up sooner or later.

I felt bad for Heidi, because it so happened that all of Rick's family were out of town when Rick disappeared. She must have felt so alone with no support from his immediate family.

There were many phone or in-person interviews by the State Troopers with family, friends, and acquaintances. I always hoped and prayed that some bit of information would be helpful. Each hour, day, and night seemed like an eternity while we waited for any news on the mysterious disappearance of my son. We had many phone calls from family and friends inquiring about any news about Rick. Finally, my husband, Tom, just told everybody that there was no need to call and that we would let them know if we heard anything new.

I kept telling Heidi that no matter where Rick was—he was in God's hands, one way or the other. That was the only comforting thought that kept me from going insane. I felt like I was hanging on by a thread. I knew I had to somehow keep it together. I had family to think of. I couldn't let myself fall apart. My grandchildren especially needed me, and they kept me going.

Heidi and I gave each other a lot of strength. We had Rick in common and we bonded so much during this time of tragedy. There would be times when I felt like I just couldn't bear it any longer, and my only consolation was to call Heidi. Sometimes I was crying so much I couldn't talk, but upon hearing her voice I would calm down.

And it was vice versa for her.

I was so grateful that Heidi's mother, Cindi, lived a short distance from her. There were several times that Cindi went over to Heidi's house in the middle of the night because Heidi was having a very difficult time. Nights were especially difficult for Heidi because when Rick came home late at night after she was in bed, she would hear his footsteps on the walkway in front of the bedroom and living room before he entered the house. Every night Heidi went through this— listening for Rick to come home. I hurt for her. I was in my own type of pain, but Heidi, as a mother to Rick's children, had to listen to her children cry for their dad. It was especially hard when it came to Calvin because he was only five years old and couldn't understand why Rick wasn't there. He just wanted his dad home. It was always a consolation when the family said their prayers before going to bed. I was grateful for our family faith. It gave us all hope and strength.

Chapter Seven

Continuing with the memories of my own experiences, immediately after I got back from our trip I went right back to work. You know, people always say, "Stay home if you need time to rest," but the fact of the matter is that if I had done that, I would have felt worse. I had to keep moving and try to keep busy. I felt like my mind and body were like mechanical machines. I went through the movements of a daily routine and tried to focus with the main part of my mind on my job, but the back of my mind was on Rick twenty-four seven.

Even though I was able to work, I wasn't mentally ready to get involved with Rick's investigation or search. It just hurt too much. Heidi and I had different strengths regarding Rick's disappearance. I was so grateful for Heidi taking the initiative to distribute posters about Rick's disappearance so soon after he went missing. She and a friend went throughout the Kenai Peninsula and with the consent of the owners, pinned up posters at businesses. Almost all the people were very kind and understanding.

There were just a couple of people who made insensitive remarks. I'm sure they weren't even aware of it. One person in particular who knew Rick's lifestyle remarked off handedly that "he probably committed suicide." This was very hurtful to hear, but Heidi handled it very diplomatically. People just don't think. For one thing, they are not in the frame of mind to feel your pain. Nevertheless, I think it's good to bring this to their attention so as to prevent any unnecessary hurt if another situation like this occurs in their future.

Heidi and I both had friends tell us (with good intentions) that if Rick had, in fact, passed on, he was in a better place. Though this was intended to be a comforting thought, it was very painful right after losing our loved one. Timing is everything. We hurt and missed him so much that all we wanted was to have him home with us.

I read in a magazine once that a mother who had just lost her daughter in a car accident was told by her friend that her daughter was at God's table. The mother's response was that she didn't want her daughter at God's table—but at *her* table! I couldn't agree more with how that mother felt at that time. I have a great love and faith in a spiritual sense, but I'm very human also. I was having many discussions with God at this time, saying that I trusted Him completely about Rick's destiny, but I still loved and missed my son immensely in the physical. God is all-understanding and it was my greatest comfort to have these open conversations with Him.

Chapter Eight

As the month of March was slowly slipping by, we kept hoping the phone would ring and the State Troopers would give us new information on Rick's disappearance. Though they were investigating the case, it wasn't a priority situation (such as a child gone missing) and I clearly understood that. So, it was very frustrating and taxing for the family to wait, day in and day out as time dragged on. Of course, all family members and friends did the best they could to inquire from any source they could think of, for any inkling of Rick's whereabouts. What really irritated me the most was when someone said that Rick could be out of state or hiding out someplace. At one point a State Trooper did mention this to a relative of mine. Anyone who really knew Rick and was close to him would never surmise this. The only possibility for this to have happened was if Rick hadn't been in his right mind for an extended period of time. The fact is, Rick would always call home no matter what! Besides that, with Rick leaving his wallet and identification in the vehicle, how in the world would he be able to travel anywhere, let alone out of the state?

One month had passed when my niece Gloria, residing in Anchorage, suggested that we get together as a family and have a meeting. I thought this was a very good suggestion. We could all share our thoughts and feelings and give moral and emotional support to each other. This suggestion by Gloria was especially appreciated by Heidi and me. My husband, Tom, initially opposed the idea because he thought (like a lot of men do) that it would just unnecessarily upset everyone, causing tears and so forth. I'm not a very patient person and this was frustrating to me because I thought just the opposite. In the end, it was a good learning experience for Tom, because he realized that it was a good idea and everyone did feel better expressing their feelings.

My brother Ray stated that he didn't believe (at this time) that Rick had expired because there was no proof or evidence. This thought did make Heidi and me feel better temporarily. We hadn't thought of it that way.

My son Troy shared that he had been informed through the grapevine that Rick had left Anchorage with an undisclosed amount of drugs. If he had used these, it would have impaired his thinking and caused disillusionment. I believe at this time Troy shared the state of mind of my brother Ray.

My nephew Pat (who was the same age as Rick) said that he would continue the search by snowmachine in the area where Rick had disappeared.

Gloria's husband, Kirk, who was a pilot, said that as soon as the snow melted in May he would search the area in his plane.

We also discussed the idea of forming a "grid" (a large group of searchers crisscrossing one another) in May when the snow was all gone. The meeting all in all went well and I think we all felt better. In my mind it was better than sitting around doing nothing. At least this way we had somewhat of a plan to further the search. It also felt good to come together as a family to support one another.

After the meeting we enjoyed a nice family dinner. I remember this as being one of those times where I felt a huge comfort. There's nothing like being surrounded by a loving and caring family in times of turmoil. I'll always appreciate my niece Gloria's suggesting this family get-together.

Chapter Nine

During this time I was feeling so much despair that I had absolutely no appetite. I would try to drink water or have a cup of coffee in the morning. I remember one evening I tried to get down a chicken wing but it was very difficult. I knew I had to always try to eat something even if it was a small portion of cream of wheat or oatmeal. It was easier to eat soft food. I lost ten pounds and got down to 102 pounds. Soup was the easiest meal to eat.

I was crying so much during the day that I carried a washcloth in my pocket sprinkled with essential oils such as lavender, which was supposed to have a calming effect. At night when in bed I put the washcloth under my pillow. That way I muffled any sobbing noise and did not draw any attention from my husband, who had the same difficulty sleeping. Actually, it was worse for Tom because he has always suffered from insomnia.

On the average, no one likes crying in front of other people. It's usually a private affair. I was no exception. I've always been able to control my tears until I was alone. But this situation with my son missing was such a deep-down emotion that I couldn't always contain my crying. I so disliked this, especially if I was in public.

I remember driving home one day, with Tom ahead of me driving his own vehicle. I thought it was safe to cry because I was alone. But when I got home Tom commented that he could see me crying when he looked out his side mirror. I tried to hide my mourning from Tom because every time he saw me cry he would try to "fix" it. This really frustrated me. I could get no relief by holding my feelings in.

One evening I was very distraught and crying. I felt so lost and flustered. I wanted so much to go see someone or go someplace to find solace. I had never experienced this type of deep pain. Previously, I had lost both my parents and a close brother, but the pain wasn't severe like what I was going through now. I kept thinking, "If only I could break a leg or arm, at least the physical pain would give me some relief from this internal hurt." My husband, who felt helpless seeing me crying, kept asking "What's wrong?" Now this might seem a ridiculous question, but he may have thought that if I could talk about it I would feel better. Like I said, I was so beside myself I just said, "I don't know!" I didn't have the energy to try and identify my intense feelings. I couldn't think of what to say or do, so I just decided to go for a drive.

I got in my car and started driving toward town. I was crying so hard that I couldn't see very well. I kept taking off my glasses to wipe my eyes. In addition, I kept putting the washcloth up to my face with the essential oil sprinkled on it so I would hopefully feel better by taking in deep breaths from it. I kept praying out loud because I felt like I was on the verge of insanity.

I was desperately praying to God to please give me the guidance and direction on what to do or where to go! I ended up at the Catholic Church in the middle of town. I drove as close as I could to the gazebo which was right next to the church. There is a huge statue of Mother Mary in the center of the gazebo.

I sat in my car looking at that gazebo and praying to Mother Mary and imploring her to please help me. Now, I wasn't praying *to* the statue, but being in that environment did help me to focus better on my prayers. I believe the energy of my surroundings gave me comfort, which you can interpret as the Holy Spirit.

After I prayed, I drove around again for some time. I was drawn to Ruth's house, an aunt of my daughter-in-law Peggy. She also lived in the middle of town. When I arrived there, I tried to communicate to her, between tears, what I was feeling and thinking. I mentioned that I was concerned about Rick's soul because of the lifestyle he had led. She already knew that I felt that Rick was deceased. Ruth listened to what I was trying to say. I could barely speak because I was feeling such agonizing emotional pain. Ruth reminded me, because we think like-minded, that when we come to this earth we sometimes choose lifestyles that may be unpleasant, but we ourselves learn our spiritual lessons from these experiences, and perhaps teach others around us these same lessons. I shared with Ruth that Rick (who was thirty-five years old at the time of his disappearance) had always said that he would die by the time he was thirty-seven. He had told friends and Heidi this same thing many times. Talking about all this to Ruth comforted me somewhat.

Ruth then asked if I would like her to do a little *Reiki* on me. The intention was to bring calming energy into my body so as to heal. I was familiar with this method of healing though I personally hadn't experienced it before. Because I had known Ruth for quite a long time and trusted her completely, I agreed to her suggestion. I was so beside myself that I was open to anything that might help me improve my state of being. Ruth had me lie down on her couch and instructed me to close my eyes and take deep breaths. She spread her hands, starting at the top of my head and very slowly moving them down the center of my body. She would stop for a short time over the charka areas, the body's energy points. I gradually started to relax enough to calm my mind somewhat, and I was able to breathe more evenly. After about thirty minutes my body and mind felt more balanced and in control. This brief healing method got me through the evening. I felt I wasn't losing my senses and was more stabilized. I was so thankful for Ruth being there for me that evening and truly felt God answered my prayers. I had been in such a desperate state of mind at the time. I don't think Ruth realized until I explained to her later just how much she helped me that night. I was able to drive home fine and went to bed more calmed down. Tom was grateful to see me. My demeanor was much improved from when I had left the house earlier. It felt good to go to bed that night feeling a little bit more at rest.

Chapter Ten

Several weeks had now gone by since Rick's disappearance. Finally, I felt like I could handle visiting the State Troopers. Heidi and I went to see Larry, one of the investigating officers. I asked him what the statistics were regarding the radius within which a person disappears and where that person would be found. He said six miles. Larry also said that many times in Alaska, because of the heavy snowfall during the winter months, bodies that had disappeared would not be discovered until spring when all the snow had melted. He said that the State Troopers would try to continue the search by snowmachine or helicopter. He believed Rick had probably succumbed to hypothermia. I encouraged him to expedite the investigation as this was so agonizing to the family, not knowing what happened to Rick!

I felt a little better after that meeting just because I was able to discuss the case and get a little bit of my input out in the open, even though we really didn't get anywhere. We all felt so desperate to get some answers. It also went through the back of my mind that it could be a long, long time before we did get any answers—if we got any at all. But I didn't want to dwell on that.

I was hoping and praying to find out something, no matter how little the information.

Various relatives and friends were also trying to find out, through the grapevine, who to connect with that could give clues about Rick's disappearance. There were many people out there who associated with Rick, but they were all mum because of the lifestyle they led. It was very frustrating. Of course, there were all kinds of rumors going around, but what the State Troopers wanted was substantiated fact, not gossip.

I remember Troy helping me feel better one sad morning at work. He said, "Mom, Rick has always been able somehow to get out of tough situations because he's a survivalist. He will know what to do or say if he's in a tight spot." My spirits were somewhat uplifted. But in the back of my mind I knew this would be true only if Rick had his full faculties. Any drugs involved would cause him to think unclearly. Still, Troy's reassuring words made me feel some comfort, and at the time I was trying to handle my unsettled emotions minute by minute, hour by hour, and day by day.

More time went by and nothing was happening. I would come home from work and light a candle at my kitchen table and try to meditate. I would pray and say, "Rick, come home if you can. Please come home." I also prayed for the white light of Christ to surround Rick no matter where he was. There was always some small hope hanging out there that there was a possibility that Rick was still alive. Like my brother Ray said, there was no proof thus far that Rick was deceased. I look back now and see that I was using this small hope to keep me going in the days immediately following Rick's disappearance. In a way, one could interpret it as "No news is good news." But thinking practically, that consolation can go on only for so long. My gut intuition was still not to fool myself, but to be honest with my feelings no matter how it hurt. But a mom is a mom, and my emotions were up and down. Even so, I was trying to sort all this out and at the same time still think reasonably.

I really felt that someone was either involved in or knew about what happened to Rick. I called Kenai Crime Stoppers and talked to a very nice officer who was truly understanding and compassionate. He explained that this case could not be listed with Crime Stoppers because there was no proof that there was actually a crime involved. He sensed my frustration and knew that I was desperately trying to find any answers I possibly could. The officer said, "I can't imagine losing a daughter or son, let alone not knowing why or where." I honestly felt this man's caring and sympathy. He suggested that I call an Anchorage radio station and perhaps I could get some results by getting the news out about Rick. When I hung up the phone I felt some peace within. One person within a large police force, handling so many different kinds of cases, had taken the time to try to reach out to me in a very caring manner. Most police officers that I have dealt with have a job to do and play a business-type role, which is very understandable for their line of work. But I will never forget that considerate gentleman. Every so often I think about how he helped me get through another hour, another day, because of the kindness he showed me.

Chapter Eleven

While all this was going on, I knew that I had to process this stressful time in as healthy a way as possible, both physically and mentally. My good friend Christine and I went on walks quite often. She is a very chatty person and this was good for me because I didn't have to do much talking. It felt therapeutic for me to hear her talk in the background since my thoughts were always on Rick.

In April, Christine, Heidi, and I signed up to take a four-week boat-rowing class the following June. My heart wasn't really in it, but I needed to focus on keeping occupied in a healthy manner. It would get me out of the house in the evenings and I would be interacting with a group of people.

In the meantime, one of the things that was beneficial to me was a library book that Peggy had given me to read. It was titled *Healing Grief—Reclaiming Life After Any Loss*, by James Van Praagh. I was familiar with this author as I had read books by him before. He is a widely acclaimed medium. This book was very uplifting and comforting to me. It was not the type of reading material that Peggy would have gotten for herself, so it was ironic that she picked this book for me. Perhaps the Spirit had a hand in this since it was very helpful to my being.

I really felt a need to visit a local therapist I had seen in the past. At one time, Rick had also, upon my suggestion, visited this same therapist. I was thankful that I could get in to see her within a short period of time after making the appointment. After I was seated on the sofa in her office, I just couldn't get any words out to even explain my visit. I was weeping and had a big pile of Kleenex on my lap before I was able to utter a few words about the reason I was there. We talked for an hour, which went by very fast. She recalled from a previous visit with Rick how he and I were very bonded. When I left her office, I felt like part of the load I was carrying was lifted from my shoulders. I did not get billed for that visit because of the involved circumstances. I appreciated this act of thoughtfulness and caring. She was one person who definitely helped in the process of moving forward, though at the time I felt I was making mini-steps.

Fortunately, at this time we had friends who had a very cozy home. Tom and I loved to escape there in the evening. When I came home from work and Tom knew I was having an especially sad and hard day, he would offer to take me to Jim and Barb's. It was like therapy for me. Their home was very warm and inviting. Even though we didn't always talk about Rick, I could feel their sense of love and compassion. I'd sit quietly on the sofa while Barb chatted away. Tom was always content to discuss fishing with Jim. He usually had one of their poodle dogs on his lap petting it. Tom loves dogs and I know this was calming for him. Since evenings were especially hard for me, it was a comfort to know that I could always go to a place with such a warm setting.

Another thing that I liked to do in the evening was to rent a movie. Now it had to be a certain type of movie. It couldn't be anything that conveyed unhappiness such as violence or death. After I explained my situation to a very nice Safeway clerk she gladly helped me find the type of movie that I was looking for. One of the best movies that she suggested was *Something's Gotta Give* with Diane Keaton and Jack Nicholson. It was a good romantic comedy movie. Tom and I both enjoyed it thoroughly.

I felt like God was always there putting people in my path to help even in small ways to assist me while I was going through this very difficult time in my life. There has always been one description for God that I used, and that one word is *love*, which is truly what I felt and what kept me going. Through God I felt hope, courage, and a never ending strength.

Chapter Twelve

Right from the beginning of Rick's disappearance I had called many people asking for prayer. I arranged to have Rick put on several prayer chains. The church affiliation made no difference to me. The support through prayer was an enormous help for me. I have always believed in the power of prayer. I also had several friends and relatives I called whenever I was having an especially bad moment. Sometimes I just had them pray over the phone with me. Other times I'd just call them up to share how I was feeling and talk through it. Almost all of these calls were long distance. At times I called Joan, the intuitive I had visited in Anchorage. I used any method of support I could think of to get me through another hour, another day. I'll never forget all the people who took time out of their day to either pray or talk to me over the phone. Often these phone calls were lengthy. I always felt uplifted. Obviously, I'm the type of person who has to let out emotions and feelings. If I try to stuff them I feel like I'm going to burst with frustration.

My husband was just the opposite. He told me at the time that he'd tell our friends to talk about anything but Rick when they were conversing with me. This was exactly the opposite of what I felt. I believed that in order for me to process this terrible ordeal I had to confront it. I know Tom thought that he was helping by trying to protect me from being hurt, but everyone has to deal with pain in his or her own way.

I attended church every week and never missed lighting a candle for Rick before Mass. When receiving communion, I inevitably became emotional and cried. It was at that time that I really felt God's love embracing me. Invariably, I felt relief, though I did not like other parishioners seeing me sobbing. I tried to be as discreet as possible by sitting far away from anyone. That is sometimes hard to do in church. I prayed earnestly that I wouldn't cry in front of people, but the heart-rending tears continually flowed.

A friend of mine told me that she had heard that Rick had visited the pastor at her church several months before he disappeared. Although my two children were baptized Catholic, I instilled in them openness to other faiths. I wanted them to have the freedom to worship or attend church wherever they felt most comfortable.

I made a phone call to this pastor and, after telling him about Rick's disappearance, made an appointment to visit with him. This pastor remembered Rick's visit vividly. Rick had been troubled and went to him at the recommendation of a friend's mother. The pastor said that Rick was very open and honest about his drug problem and had admitted his shortcomings. They had prayed together before Rick left. The pastor said that he had seen Rick's Missing Person poster and had put it in his office so that he would always remember to pray for him. This man was very warm-hearted and I so appreciated the time he took with Rick. Before we concluded our visit, we prayed together. I was consoled by this meeting and quietly thanked God for putting someone in my path once again to get me through another day.

Chapter Thirteen

It was very painful to see Rick's kids bear this ordeal. I felt their confusion. They missed their Dad immensely and just wanted him to come home. In their child minds they were trying to understand the whole situation. Every night they prayed with Heidi for Rick's safe return. Children have so much faith. Heidi felt so helpless when they cried for their Dad. She had no answers for them except for the consolation of prayer.

Rosie and Calvin wrote poems about their Dad which touched all of our hearts. Rosie's poem is as follows:

HUGS AND KISSES

I like to hug my Dad
I sometimes like to give him a kiss

But now that he's gone, I can't
And I really, really miss him

I remember when we used to go fishing
Now I'm wishing he was here so we could go fishing

He will always be in my heart – My Dad

Rosie confided to her Mom that Rick appeared to her one night in her bedroom after she had gone to bed. (This happened shortly after Rick had disappeared.) She said that Rick was standing by the window in his blue jeans and winter coat. Rosie said that she became a little scared but was trying to be brave. After she told her mom about it, Heidi assured her not to be afraid and to tell her dad that she loved him if ever it happened again. As it turned out she did see him one more time. She was spending the night with her aunt Jesse when Rick appeared by the door of the bedroom. She did as her mom had advised and told him that she loved him.

Rosie was very spiritually minded even at age eight. During that same time, she and her aunt Jesse were watching a TV program about fathers giving away their daughters on their wedding day. Rosie turned to her aunt and asked in a very emotional manner, "Who will give me away on my wedding day?" Aunt Jesse replied, "Why, of course your dad will, Rosie." Rosie replied, "But he is in spirit!" Her aunt Jesse was at a loss for words.

Calvin's poem is just as touching.

I LOVE MY DAD

Me and my Dad went for a ride in his truck
The weather was good, so we were in luck

We went to his friend's house to play his guitar and drums

When we were finished we went to the store. He bought me a toy.

These are some of my favorite things I remember about my DAD!

I recalled what my sister-in-law Clare had told me regarding the last Christmas Rick was with his family. Rick had driven to Anchorage to Christmas-shop for Heidi and the kids. After purchasing the presents he drove to Palmer, where Archie and Clare lived. Clare was impressed and touched when he showed her all the gifts he had picked out. He wanted to wrap them there so that all the presents would be ready to go under the tree when he walked into the house. I remember the kids being tickled with all their Christmas presents.

I also recalled the previous summer when Rick asked me to go fishing with him and the kids. We loaded the fishing box, poles, and snacks into his truck and drove to one of the many Kenai River banks. The pinks were running so the kids caught a lot of fish. Rick was very patient with them though they often got the fishing lines all tangled up. The kids had a blast and I had fun watching them.

One of the most memorable times I spent with Rick, Heidi, and the kids was when we went sledding at one of the high schools earlier that winter. We had these huge rubber tubes that we all piled onto and went sliding down the hill at a very fast rate. We laughed all the harder when we crashed at the bottom of the hill! After sledding we usually went back to my house and had a big dinner. I loved family togetherness.

It was January 2004, about one month before Rick went missing, when Heidi, Rick, the kids, and I all drove up to Palmer to spend a couple of days visiting Archie and Clare. Archie had just gotten a pool table for his birthday in December. Rick and Calvin played pool, though Calvin wasn't much taller than the pool table. How cute it was to see him try to play even though he was only five years old.

The next day we all went snowmachining, since Archie and Clare owned several machines and lived on a very open area of forty acres. I took Mackenzie with me since she was timid about riding alone. Heidi and Rosie went together. Rosie has a brave demeanor and didn't mind going fast at all. I saw Rick and Calvin at one point going across the field like bats out of hell, and I surely was glad that it was a family rule to always wear helmets! We all crashed a few times but that's the fun of snowmachining.

I think back of these fun times and thank the Lord for warm memories!

Chapter Fourteen

I n May 2004 Heidi and I had 500 posters about Rick's disappearance printed and distributed with the local newspaper. It was to be a weekend delivery so that there would be more reader exposure. It was an 8-by-11 poster with two different pictures of Rick, with the word "M I S S I N G" in large letters on top. There was a description of Rick along with the message stating: "Last seen February 25, 2004 in Sterling, Alaska. Please call the State Troopers." There was also a reward available to individuals with information directly leading to the location of Rick Hills. Every time we had posters distributed, we had high hopes that someone would call with any bit of information. It kept us going and we felt like we were doing *something*! Even though everyone had jobs to go to daily, it felt like we were just sitting and waiting. It was agonizing, but we had no choice but to do our best to keep moving on and *hope* that some bit of news would come forward.

Mother's Day of May, 2004, was an especially heart-wrenching day for me. I had saved one of the few cards I had gotten from Rick for Mother's Day. This one was from May 2001. He had sent it from the Wildwood Pre-Trial Facility in Kenai where he was at the time (because of some traffic violations). I had kept the card because it meant a lot to me. First, Rick *thought* of me, and second, for what the card said. The front had three pretty red roses and said, "For a Wonderful Mom," and the inside read "With loving thanks for all you've done . . . for all you do . . . happy Mother's Day" and was signed, "Lots of Love, your son Rick." I kept this card above my desk at work and it had always warmed me to occasionally glance up and look at it.

This Mother's Day was a warm, sunny day, so I planned to do something that would be comforting. I asked my youngest granddaughter, Danielle, who was five at the time, to help me plant flowers. We were home and alone. It was quiet and peaceful. Danielle was good company. Just being around a grandchild and feeling her love was very consoling.

Also in May of that year Heidi and I drove Rosie and Calvin out to the Sterling area, where Rick had disappeared, to physically look for him. Now this may seem odd since it had been three months from the time Rick had disappeared. Heidi's intentions were to provide solid memories for the children that they were involved in the search for their father. It was a sunny day and we walked mainly in the ditch off the roads looking in culverts and in the surrounding dense trees and underbrush. Again, for me it felt like we were actively doing something. Calvin had turned six years old that month and I know in his young mind he hoped that we would find his dad just like when he had last seen him. As we were driving on the way home from Sterling, Calvin said "I really hoped to find my dad today. I really prayed that we would, but . . . " then he halfway shrugged his shoulders as if to indicate "it just didn't happen." It was times like these that my heart would just go out to him. He had such faith for being so young. I tried my best to give a response that would somehow comfort my grandchildren during occurrences like these, but it never felt adequate. I wanted to remove their hurt as much as possible, though I realized that each one of us in the family had to process our pain in our own way, no matter what the age. The best comfort that I could give my loved ones was to share with them as much love as possible and to give encouragement to keep their faith strong through prayer. Rosie and Calvin had a very strong faith for their age and I will always feel very fortunate and appreciate Heidi for instilling this confidence and trust in them.

Chapter Fifteen

June 1, 2004 was an extremely hard day for me. I was at work and entering payroll in the computer for approximately fifty employees. The date of each check was June 4, which was the date of Rick's birthday. He would have been thirty-six years old. Each time I entered data for a check and punched in that date, I became emotional and cried very hard, but at the same time tried to hold it in because I was at work. Fortunately, the other employees were in different rooms. I was earnestly praying to keep my sanity. I remember I kept repeating, "Why, God, why?!" I wanted some answers so bad—to keep from going nuts. Payroll took me most of the day but somehow I got through it.

At one point I went outside behind the building just to get away for a break. I entered the carport that Rick had constructed for the business the previous fall. I happened to look up at the tin roof and saw that Rick had sprayed his name "Rick Hills" on one of the pieces of material roofing that he had purchased. I recognized his printing and felt a hard twinge of pain in my heart. Here I was—trying to run from my pain only to fall face first into it again. I talked to God again . . . "Is this supposed to comfort me, knowing that Rick is here with me in spirit, if not in the physical?" Or, "I cannot run from the pain, I have to somehow process this no matter how long it takes"? Or maybe it was yes to both questions. I hurt so much I really didn't know if I was coming or going. But at the same time I was trying to keep my sanity.

During the month of June I took the boat-rowing class that I had signed up for in April with Heidi and Christine. I was grateful that it was in the evenings because the nights were a difficult time for me. Most of the time when I was at the class I had a hard time focusing. But I knew I had to keep busy doing something. The mosquitoes were very bad and a lot of the time the weather wasn't the greatest, but it got me out and around people. My heart continually hurt because my mind was nearly always focused on Rick. I asked myself so many times, "What in the *hell* am I doing out here anyway?" Once the class got to the point where we entered the boats in the water and actually started rowing, the physical aspect of it felt good. If nothing else, it was a good stress release.

During the first part of June, a friend of mine suggested that I contact a Shamanic healer for whom she had a high personal regard. Zoe was very intuitive and could help me make contact with Rick through a metaphysical process. I knew that this would finalize any question in my mind about Rick being "on the other side." It was something that I knew I had to eventually do for myself, but I didn't want to act too fast because I felt that I just needed to give it some time before I made contact with Rick. I needed to try to keep moving forward and I knew this would help me. I contacted Zoe, who resided out of state, and made an appointment for June 10 for a reading. She suggested I light a candle and pray about the upcoming reading, as she also would be doing. I did as she proposed. As the time neared, my emotions were stirred, but I tried to keep them in control.

Finally, the appointed time arrived, and I was very much looking forward to the conversation. Zoe relayed to me that she saw Rick traveling down a road fast in a truck, like he was being chased. She said it was snowing. Then she saw him walking and his feet were cold. At that point Rick himself spoke up. The first thing he said was that he was sorry for all the sorrow he had caused. Fighting tears, I replied "You're one hundred percent forgiven!" His response was "You're a wonderful mom!" I knew Rick was saying this to verify that it was actually him communicating. "You're a wonderful Mom" was on the Mother's Day card he had previously given me. I had kept it above my desk at work. Rick, through Zoe, stated that it was his destiny to pass on and that his death had been nonviolent. He had work to do on the astral plane and when the time was right he would contact me. Rick said his foot was better and he wasn't limping anymore. He laughingly said that he was being productive for a change, by helping little kids not to get involved in drugs. He also said that he was trying to help Troy and Tom deal with his passing on. He stated that Tom's feelings of pain were buried very deep. Rick also said that he was concerned about his children and that he had appeared to Rosie because it was easy to make contact with her, unlike Heidi, whose head was like a whirlwind. Rick did have a good connection with me. I was trying to keep my emotional pain under control but did manage to say, "Thank you for being my son for thirty-five years." His response was, "I'm still your son!" In other words, nothing had changed just because he was not in the physical anymore. He was *still* Rick, though in the spirit world. I appreciated those words so much.

I was glad I hadn't given any information to Zoe about Rick, except for the fact that he had disappeared. That way it was verified to me that it was actually Rick with whom I was communicating, because only he and I knew the information we were discussing.

I felt bittersweet relief after that conversation—making contact with Rick and knowing that he was in a good place, but also finalizing that he was no longer with us on the earthly plane.

Chapter Sixteen

Later, during the third week of June, Heidi and I had an appointment with Joan in Anchorage to see if any more information would be revealed through her, in reference to the circumstances of Rick's disappearance. Joan felt that Rick's body was perhaps in the Kenai River in the area about a mile directly from the airstrip where his last tracks were traced. She also candidly asked Rick out loud in front of Heidi and me, "Rick, how did your passing over go?" His response was "It was a piece of cake!" That put a grin on our faces. You would think that if Rick answered an open question like that, why wouldn't he give us the exact details of his disappearance. Like Joan said, she never knows what a spirit is going to reveal but there's a reason for everything. I do believe that God's timing is perfect, though it was very tough for me to be patient. I wanted answers because this mystery of Rick was so agonizing to all of his loved ones. Our suffering would somewhat subside if we had some type of closure.

After Heidi and I returned to Soldotna I contacted one of my nephews who had a boat and motor and arranged for the three of us to search the Kenai River in the area of the Kenai Keys. Since this was the third week of June, the river was quite high. Joan suggested we look around an island in the middle of the river. The island was fairly flooded. We spent a lot of time looking for any of Rick's clothing and so on that could have been snagged on rocks or trees. I wanted to find some kind of evidence so badly, though I was half scared we would discover something that would be hard to look at. Of course, I was praying all the while we were on our search. This excursion gave me hope, though it was also disappointing that we didn't find anything. Heidi and I felt like we were doing something. It was so hard to just sit by and wait. I talked to some relatives about forming a grid in the area where Rick disappeared, but was discouraged from doing so for some reason or other. In hindsight, I wish (in a way) that I had followed my intuition to do so. But, as I have stated before, God's timing isn't our timing and everything happens for a reason.

Another type of search we undertook was flying over the area in a buck-eye (a motorized para-glider that seats two people). My friend Christine's husband, Doug, owned one and was glad to be of help by taking Tom up to fly over the area all along the river and vast tundra terrain. Even though you don't travel as fast as in an airplane, it's still difficult to see anything in detail.

Also, Tom and I had both flown over the area with my niece's husband, Kirk, in his plane. I then understood what Tom was talking about when he said it was like looking for a needle in a haystack when searching from the air.

I always hoped and prayed for any sign or discovery that would give us some answers in our search for Rick.

I also requested prayer from relatives and friends, for the family to receive closure on Rick, by finding his body. Any time I conferred with the police or was involved with a physical search for Rick, I became drained in body and mind from praying so hard and having high hopes for getting some answers. By the end of the day I felt very weak. An adrenaline rush can be a survival tool, but when you come down off it, you fall flat on your face.

Tom could see this happening so he didn't like it when I got my hopes so high. He didn't want to see me disappointed when there was no outcome on these occasions. But Tom and I are two different people and we handled and viewed everything in the opposite way. I appreciated Tom the way he was because he helped keep me somewhat balanced and grounded with his quiet demeanor and common sense. We so needed to hold each other up!

Chapter Seventeen

Heidi and I continued to keep in touch with Joan for any ongoing information. She gave us three pertinent names that came to her that were related to the area where Rick disappeared. She told us to check them out. We relayed this information to the State Troopers, knowing that they might not be open to intuitive information. There was no factual basis or evidence. I was now somewhat emotionally stronger, so I could go in and talk more frequently with the investigators. This in contrast to the beginning, when I was just hoping to have the case solved without having to get involved. But as time went by and nothing seemed to be moving forward (except at a crawl) I figured I'd just better roll up my sleeves and push onward to try and get some answers. I've always believed in the adage "God helps those who help themselves." There was one particular sergeant I met with who was helpful. He had received a number of calls regarding Rick's disappearance and had to check them all out for any leads. He even met in disguise with a supposed informant at an undisclosed location. The sergeant was told the whereabouts of Rick's body. But the information was unreliable because the informant appeared to be flaky and disoriented.

The State Troopers questioned many people, including one of the three pertinent people Joan had suggested we check out. That one person had an alibi at the time of Rick's disappearance. I had strongly urged a particular lieutenant to give this person, who happened to be involved in drugs, a lie detector test. He said he couldn't do that even if that person was a likely suspect unless it was agreed upon. I stated that if a person had nothing to hide, why wouldn't he or she agree to a lie detector test? The lieutenant said, "Look, Mrs. Hills, not everybody who is a drug addict is a bad person." I said, "I know that, my son Rick was involved with drugs!" This lieutenant also stated that he was a skeptic regarding any information from an intuitive. This is understandable because his line of work is based on physical evidence. But I told the lieutenant to put himself in my desperate position and to imagine having a missing son or daughter and having no leads to go on; you would turn to anything or anyone that just might be helpful. He agreed.

During that summer, one of Rick's close friends stopped by my office. He wanted to pass on some information he had heard while recently serving a short time in the correctional facility in Kenai. There had been a lot of talk among inmates regarding the person I had wanted the State Troopers to give the lie detector test to. Rick's friend stated that everyone thought this person was involved with Rick's mysterious disappearance. I thanked him for the information but told him that he needed to inform the State Troopers about it. They would want firsthand knowledge. Several people had forwarded information to the State Troopers but unfortunately, nothing came of it. Perhaps they needed more substantial evidence, or maybe Rick's case was put on the back burner because of more prioritized cases. Also, I realized that some of Rick's friends or acquaintances were afraid to be involved because of their shady backgrounds, and they were fearful of being exposed because it could be harmful to them. It was very frustrating to Heidi and me.

Then one afternoon while I was driving back to work after a lunch break, I received a very serious sounding phone call from Joan. She said it came to her that Rick had, in fact, passed on as a result of head trauma. A lot of thoughts passed through my mind simultaneously. I recalled my previous phone call with Zoe when Rick had relayed that his death was nonviolent. It also crossed my mind that whatever had actually happened to Rick didn't change the fact that he was gone and I knew in my heart that he was now in a better place where he was at peace. I still became my emotional self, but prayed very earnestly to get through these painful moments. Through tears, as I was driving down the road, I knew God heard my prayers asking for strength. Losing a son was a totally new experience for me and I was trying to hold myself together to the best of my ability.

My focus was to find Rick's body so that the family could have closure and therefore move on. I fervently prayed for this. I'm a very determined person once I make up my mind about something and I don't give up easily. I knew that I would continue to exhaust every possible avenue to get answers!

Chapter Eighteen

As the summer of 2004 rolled by I reminisced about Rick doing his seasonal "thing"—commercial fishing every year at Bristol Bay, mainly in the Naknek and Dillingham areas. Rick started commercial fishing at the age of fourteen. My family is originally from the Bristol Bay area and our main income was commercial fishing. It was in Rick's blood to continue with this type of vocation. He started out working for my older sister, Judy, on several set net sites. During his high school years he fished for my older brother, Ray, on a commercial fishing boat. In his later years he captained his own boat. Rick was a very hard worker and did well at commercial fishing, whether the season was productive or not. He also loved sport fishing, and had a natural instinct about how to fish and where to fish. I believe this is when Rick had the most peace in his life.

I recalled late one summer evening when he stopped by and told Tom and me he was taking Heidi and Mack down the Russian River in a rowboat for some fishing and sightseeing. Heidi and Mack said that was one of the best outings they had experienced. Not only was the fishing enjoyable, but they had seen a black bear on the bank while drifting down the river.

I also thought back to a couple of occasions when Rick got me up in the early morning hours to take a thirty-minute drive to the Kasilof River to fish for reds off the bank. I laughed when the guide boats going by saw Rick pulling in a fish, when their clients, fishing in the same spot off the boat, didn't catch anything. It didn't look good for the guides, especially when the clients pointed at Rick with envy. We could hear them say, "What's that guy doing that we're not?!"

Typically, I gave up fishing after about an hour and Rick could keep going forever. It was the time that Rick could truly relax and feel like he was in seventh heaven. It was especially enjoyable because the atmosphere was fairly quiet. You could hear the birds chirp or a fish jump and hear the ripple of the water. Experiencing this natural environment has a very calming effect. To me it's like being one with God. These memories with Rick will always be held in my heart in a special way.

On many occasions Rick went drift fishing, either on the Russian or Kenai River, with Troy and Kurt. All three loved fishing. We laughed when we'd later hear that Kurt often had to be a mediator between Rick and Troy doing their brotherly squabbling. Rick and Troy were only eleven months apart, but they were like night and day. They both had a sense of humor but that was different, too. Their difference in personalities made parental life interesting for me. *Most* of the time it was enjoyable!

It was not uncommon during the summer or fall months to see Rick jump on Heidi's bike to ride from their house to the "Big Eddy" fishing hole. He would throw the bike in some bushes and proceed to fish off the bank of the Kenai River. He either went in the wee hours of the morning or late at night. Heidi said he always came home with a plastic garbage sack full of fish.

Rick used to do this same thing as a kid. One summer at around age eleven, Rick was staying with his uncle Rob, because Tom and I were out of town and he needed to attend summer school for a couple of weeks. In the morning hours he'd ride his bike two miles to Slikok Creek on K-Beach road and throw his bike in the bushes while he fished. That worked fine for a while until his bike got stolen while he was fishing! Even at that, I remember him still catching a ten- to twelve-pound king salmon and proudly bringing it back to Rob's in a plastic garbage bag!

One of my recent favorite pictures taken is of Rick holding a nice-size three- or four-pound rainbow trout that he had caught on the upper Kenai River during the fall. He released the fish, of course, but had the picture taken because it was a nice catch. You can see the pride in his vivacious grin! Fishing was truly a major enjoyment that Rick embraced in life.

Chapter Nineteen

I continued to reach out to any and all to pray for closure on Rick. I have a close friend, Janet, who lives in Bakersfield, California. I was communicating with her by fax from my place of work. I constantly asked her and her family for prayer. Her two girls were close to the same age as my kids and had grown up together in their earlier years. Janet's encouraging words always gave comfort to me. She always reminded me that they loved us dearly and were praying long and hard for closure on Rick. Corresponding by fax to my dear friend was so convenient, especially if I was having a bad day while at work. I could slip a few words on paper about my thoughts and Janet would receive it in a few minutes at her place of employment. In reflection, supportive ways like this so enabled me to keep going!

I was very grateful for my network of family and friends that I would reach out to in time of need. Most connections were via phone since I worked most of the time and was alone at my office. I was never shy to pick up the phone and make that call. One of the people I conversed with often was a very compassionate mother of six who lived in Bristol Bay, the area where I was raised as a child. This lady was very understanding and patient.

She would listen and was open to everything I had to say. She was Catholic and very spiritual. I always felt better after talking to her. Another person was a childhood friend named Rhonda who lived in Anchorage. When I felt a need for prayer I would call her or my sister V.V., who lived in Oregon. They would pray with me over the phone anytime I called. One time, I even phoned a friend of Rick's at a church in Kenai. Rick at one time had attended that church and had confided in me that the congregation had laid hands on him in prayer, and that he had gotten very emotional. I was glad to hear that because I knew that the Holy Spirit had touched him.

Yet I was still very depressed and sad. My heart felt heavy. It actually felt like it was broken into a million pieces if you can understand that. I called my sister Liz in Alabama one day on my way home from work. I pulled over in a parking lot so that I would have sole focus on the conversation. I asked Liz how in the world she handled the deaths of *three* sons out of the six children that were born to her. She said many times she felt like giving up, but she had to live for her remaining children and grandchildren. We also talked about when our own mother had lost a son (referred to always by the nickname Bumbum).

Bumbum died at the age of thirteen through a drowning in the Kvichak River, up from the village of Levelock where we lived at the time. He was boating with my sister Judy and her husband. Bumbum had fallen overboard and was yelling for Judy to help him. When she jumped in the swift water to try and help my brother, the undercurrent was so strong it pulled them both under. Judy was drowning when she saw a piece of string (or so she thought) in front of her. She grabbed it and held on for dear life. It was actually a rope that her husband had thrown to her, thus saving her life. We never did find my brother's body, though the river was searched by many.

This was my closest brother at the time. They didn't have support groups in those days, and as I look back I really felt for my mother because neither she nor the rest of the family received closure on my brother's death. As I was growing up I heard my mother say, more than once, "One of the worst things that can happen to a parent is when a child dies before them." Now I can fully understand the impact of those words. It felt like history was repeating itself. I was in the same situation as my mother once was. Perhaps my son Rick was in the river, and I too wanted so desperately to find his body. Then we all would have closure and receive some relief. But so far it wasn't to be.

I was so despondent during the summer following my son's disappearance that the future looked and felt dismal to me. I thought I would try to seek medical help. A relative of mine suggested I make an appointment with a doctor who was licensed to practice both medicine and psychology. When I walked into her office and she questioned the nature of my visit, I couldn't get any words out. There was a big lump in my throat and after about five minutes and a dozen attempts, I finally got the message across. I started out by saying in a low and quiet tone with my head bowed, "I'm so sorrowful . . ." After listening, and in reply to her questions, she stated that I seemed to be doing all the right things to help myself in handling the situation. I asked if I could get a prescription for the lowest dosage available for an antidepressant. I felt like I needed a boost or a little kick in the butt to get me moving uphill, so to speak. She complied and said that it would take a little while for the medicine to work. Just talking to this lady helped a lot, even though it seemed it was just in the moment. I realized that when I walked out of her office, I would be leaving a cocoon of compassion and understanding. After a day or two I told my husband that I felt better. He said it was all in my head because it takes a week or so for the anti-depressant to work. I really didn't care, because even feeling a little better, whether I imagined it or not, was good. I don't think I even finished taking that prescription.

I was learning that support can come in many ways. One day while I was at the post office, I bumped into an older friend of mine who had previously lost a daughter through an auto accident. The daughter was the mother of three small children. I asked him how he handled his loss. His response was, "Dolly, the pain doesn't ever go away, but it gets easier with time." This made sense to me. His words gave me strength to cope with the loss of my son.

Chapter Twenty

Time passed in a blur. It was late summer and Heidi and I decided to have another 500 posters of Rick's disappearance printed. We arranged to have them distributed via the local newspaper. They were inserted in the paper and delivered in the most heavily populated areas. I found it surprising that a couple of people called after receiving the paper stating that they hadn't heard about Rick and were shocked to hear the news. I always hoped that if somebody out there knew about, or was connected in any way with Rick's disappearance, would *feel a need* to come forward with this substantial information. These hopes and anticipations helped me to keep moving forward.

In August 2004 I contacted Joan, the first intuitive I had reached out to. I told her that I had been working with a sergeant from the State Troopers office who was open to the information she had so far conveyed. I also had been talking to a young man who was a detective on Rick's case. I liked both of these officers because I felt they were genuinely interested in solving this ongoing investigation.

During the first week of October I arranged for Joan and the detective to go with Heidi and me to check out the river on the Kenai Keys. I felt this was urgent because it was getting cold, and ice could start forming in the river. I had a good friend take us in his motorized skiff. We were hoping we could find any shred of evidence, such as clothing, along the shoreline. (I was praying, *desperately,* to find something, even if it was Rick's body). I was hopeful that with Joan present, she would be able to contribute some insight into the search. I felt physically and emotionally drained after this excursion on the river, but also somewhat consoled by trying to do *something* to get *somewhere.* I had to keep trying. Heidi shared these feelings. Tom, on the other hand, would see me get my hopes up only to see them dashed after the disappointing results.

Yes, it would seem at times I was going on a wild goose chase, but, as I have said before, it was better than sitting home and doing nothing. That really would have driven me nuts. Also, as a mother who was so emotionally involved, I acted differently than Tom, who kept his feelings inside. I, like most mothers, would go above and beyond when it came to my children, no matter the age of that child. Tom's hurt was just as deep as mine, we just reacted differently. We both felt like part of ourselves died right along with Rick. We had this family unit and now a piece of it was missing and things wouldn't be the same. We realized an adjustment to this broken family would be a long time coming.

I also asked the State Troopers if it would be possible for them to put a team together and search the Kenai River in the area where Joan thought Rick's body might be located. I surmised that they would use a large net or some other sort of contraption from a skiff, similar to the way the search had gone for my drowned brother in the Kvichak River. The State Troopers stated that I would have to contact the Central Emergency Services to perform that task. Their duties included fire and paramedic services but they were also trained in search and rescue operations. It took some time to produce results. CES first had to receive permission from the Chief, because this undertaking would involve overtime. The task would have to be performed after regular work hours or on the weekend. We also had to wait for them to fit this into their schedule. I was elated when I got word that the search was approved. I prayed in earnest that CES would have a successful search. For the family the not knowing and waiting was wretched. I prepared myself to accept the outcome of the search, whether the results were the way I wished them or not. In the back of my mind I held onto the thoughts that God's timing is perfect in all things, though I may not always understand. I had to hold on to my faith.

After we found out that the CES river search did not produce results, Heidi and I talked to the two searchers involved. They showed us the device they used to search the river for Rick's body. It was a long pole with a large hook at the end. Heidi was very disappointed in the device that was used. Like I said before, I figured that something along the lines of a net would be used because a broader area would be covered. Nonetheless the searchers stated that they worked for several hours using the pole and hook back and forth across the river in the area that we had suggested they look. Despite the results, I really appreciated the efforts of CES. These men were very sympathetic and were sorry that they didn't find anything. They were very kind and I told them we were extremely grateful that they took the time after their normal work hours to do this search.

I was always glad that I pushed forward in that direction to search the river. Finally, I could put that behind me. But *now* what?

Chapter Twenty-One

I may have given the impression that I lean toward being a religious person. Actually, I'm more of a spiritualist because of my religious beliefs. I do cuss on occasion and like to drink beer! My girlfriend Janet from Bakersfield shared this thought with me after hearing it from a preacher: We make a mistake "thinking" we are natural people trying to live a spiritual life but the truth is we are spiritual beings from God having a brief natural experience. My husband, Tom, has always said that his church was being on the water boating or fishing or out walking in the woods observing animals or birds. He loves nature and he's always at peace when he's in that space. That's about as close to God as you can be in my perspective. I always give Tom my blessing whenever he wants to go hunting or fishing because I know that this is when he feels most at ease and contented, especially if he has time alone and it is quiet.

In September 2004 Tom went on his annual Yukon moose-hunting trip up north. He towed his twenty-foot boat by truck up through Fairbanks to the Haul Road, then on to the Yukon River at the Alaska Pipeline crossing. It's about 700 miles from Soldotna. Then he travels approximately five hundred miles by boat to the mouth of the Koyokuk River and goes another 120 miles to set up moose camp. This takes three to five days, depending upon weather and how limited his time is. He's typically gone from ten to fourteen days. Tom loves this trip. It's very enjoyable because he's totally away from the hubbub of daily life. He has a hunting partner, but he always likes to go alone in the woods to moose call or just admire all the wild animals he encounters, including bear and different types of birds. He also spends a lot of time fishing for pike and sheefish.

I was glad when autumn came so Tom would go on this hunting trip. I felt it would be healing for him to get away from all the sadness and stress around the house. And I'm sure it was good for both of us to be away from each other for a while. I needed that time alone to feel free to grieve without concerning myself with Tom worrying about how I was faring.

My daughter-in-law Peggy printed out a bible scripture for Tom before he went on this hunting trip. I thought it was very appropriate for him. I loved that verse so much I kept it in sight at home and at my place of work. I would like to share this verse here because it had such an impact on me and has carried me through many minutes, hours, and days when I just felt like I couldn't go on anymore:

Philippians 4:6-8: "Don't worry about anything; instead pray about everything; tell God your needs and don't forget to thank Him for the answers. If you do this you will experience God's peace, which is far more wonderful than the human mind can understand.

His peace will keep your thoughts and your hearts quiet and at rest as you trust in Christ Jesus."

This verse was a constant reminder to me to be fully aware God does not make mistakes and to have complete faith in Him. This was easier said than done during the ordeal our family was going through, but I had to *believe* that this situation was totally in God's hands. As human beings we may not always understand why we are put through these trials and tribulations on earth. I have always felt that where we can't, God *can* see the big picture. We are like little kids growing up and having to trust in our parent Father God, who has immeasurable love for each and every one of us. This belief may not work for everybody but it sure worked for me!

Chapter Twenty-Two

At the end of October, because of the continuing unresolved disappearance of my son, along with extensive, stressful hours at work, I felt like I was at the end of my rope. I had to figure out what to do to keep from having a complete nervous breakdown, which was where I felt I was heading. I suggested to Tom that both of us take a week off from work and use our air miles to fly to Phoenix, where Tom's younger brother had a house. We would then rent a car and go on a road trip to Alabama where my older sister, Liz, resided during winter. That would be a seven-hundred-mile course of travel and we had only a week to accomplish this! Everybody was suggesting we fly straight to Alabama for more time to visit, but that wasn't my purpose. My intention was to just get in a car and drive. I wanted to get away from everybody and everything to try to get my head on straight. Like I stated previously, I was so stressed that I was rigid, like a piece of wood. I've always had a vibrant personality and love to laugh. Well, I hadn't done that in months, and truthfully, I couldn't imagine ever feeling like that again. Heidi, and many friends, were concerned because *Dolly wasn't Dolly anymore.* I couldn't even fake a laugh or smile. The only thing that really warmed me somewhat was being surrounded by my grandchildren.

Tom readily agreed to take me on this road trip. After arriving in Phoenix, we rented a car and immediately got on the road because of our limited time. We had to travel north to reach the Interstate. Well, it had started snowing and there were vehicles and trucks sliding all over the road and into the ditches. Fortunately, being from snowy country, Tom did a good job, knowing how to keep the car on the road while driving through snowing slush. This was quite stressful, but after several hours we got into decent weather, and the rest of the trip was good traveling.

After three days on the road I was still very uptight. Tom chatted and it seemed like I was a hundred miles away, always looking straight ahead. I was trying to unwind but it wasn't working. I was so tense I couldn't even focus on praying.

Then a miracle happened! It was really like a miracle to me. As Tom was driving along on the freeway, we were traveling on an open stretch with acres of green grass and huge and luscious trees on both sides of the road. It was quite picturesque. For some reason, I turned my head to the far right of me and saw a huge billboard positioned so the opposite traffic had a good view of it. Tom was driving at a fast rate of speed but I got a fairly long glimpse of this gigantic painting of Jesus with his hands extended. In large letters was the scripture "Fear not, I am with Thee." I can't even come close to describing the elated feeling that came over me! It was like Jesus was personally talking to me. I felt it!

My mind and body immediately became relaxed. I was like an icicle melting. I wanted to stay in that moment forever. I genuinely knew Spirit was giving me a message that God was always with me no matter how alone and abandoned I may have felt in these past stressful and tiring months. After that brief and enormous cloud of love and warmth enveloped me, I knew I would somehow survive the upcoming months. This all occurred in an area that is referred to as the Bible Belt. It truly was a spiritual experience. I felt so enlightened. It's difficult to put into words the overwhelming emotion I was processing at the time.

Needless to say, the remainder of the trip was enjoyable. We had never traveled that far south before and it was nice to see new country. My sister Liz and her husband, Doug, were delighted to see us. We went out to a great smorgasbord and thoroughly enjoyed the great southern food for our evening meal. We stayed only one night but had a wonderful short visit. The next day we started back to Phoenix on a different route and viewed more new country. We were in sunny Phoenix only a day or so before we had to fly back to Alaska.

Departing Phoenix, we boarded an evening flight and the plane was not very full. I was grateful for that because I went to the back of plane and had three seats to myself so I could stretch out. I wanted to be by myself. I craved being alone and unnoticed so I could grieve in privacy. I knew I needed to do this. It was like my being was swelled up with tears internally, and I had to release them. I cried all the way back to Alaska that night. Tom wasn't aware of this and I was glad because he would have tried to fix it and that wasn't what I needed. I talked to God and I talked with Rick. My heart ached, and in turn my body ached. I believe I was trying to let go, but was having a difficult time doing it. This was all a new experience to me and I was trying to learn to process it. I didn't realize at the time just how long and difficult it was going to be to let it all go.

Chapter Twenty-Three

U pon returning from our road trip during the first week of November, I felt so much better. The trip was a reprieve and I felt like I could cope for the time being. This new experience was a minute-by-minute, day-by-day effort to cope. But I reminded myself that this situation I was placed in had a purpose unknown to me. I didn't fully understand it, although I did have the faith to keep moving forward as best I could. Thank God!

On the Saturday following Thanksgiving, the yearly Christmas tree festivity was held in the city of Kenai, only ten miles from Soldotna. It's held in the evening, which adds to the excitement because of all the bright, colorful Christmas lights. After a very boisterous parade down Main Street, the lighting of a huge Christmas tree takes place in downtown Kenai. The area is always crowded with families, including their dogs, which makes it more fun. There's a lot of food and beverages available from all the different vendors participating. Traditional holiday music is played over the loudspeaker, which just adds excitement to the season. I never tire of the song "Jingle Bells" during the Christmas season. It always lifts my spirit.

Heidi and the kids and I piled into Rick's truck and drove to Kenai to enjoy these festivities. The fireworks that were displayed during the last part of the evening were the highlight of the event. The bursting array of rainbow colors along with the combustible noises, was phenomenal against the darkness of the winter evening. This beautiful scene continued for about thirty minutes. The kids jumped out of the truck and made snow angels on the ground since the snow was so fluffy. Heidi brought a thermos full of hot chocolate, which always hits the spot on a cool winter night. It was nice for everyone to be distracted for a while from the sadness that surrounded us, knowing that this would be the first Christmas Rick would not be with us.

Shortly after this pre-Christmas event, Heidi and I made arrangements with Zoe for a telephone appointment at Heidi's house with all the kids present. She was the intuitive that I had contacted in June. She asked us to meditate and pray beforehand, which Heidi and I did.

Rick came through via Zoe and stated that he missed all of us in the physical and that he was there with us at the Christmas tree lighting. He was happy to see all our smiling faces. He told me not to suffer, and though he said this was hard, it was part of the spiritual evolution. Rick said my strength came from my faith, and prayers really helped, and that Tom sees this through me and it rubs off on him. Rick also said that my emotional and spiritual bond was very powerful and that he was very involved with me, even more than before. He told the kids, in honor of him for Christmas, to give a gift to others, such as participating in the Fred Meyer Christmas tree for kids. Rick mentioned the kids individually and had something to say personally about each one as he also did for Heidi. He said that he loved talking to all of us, though we did not need to go through Zoe to do so.

It warmed me to hear that he was trying to find a cat for Rosie because she had wanted one ever since they had lost their brown cat. I got a big kick out of Heidi when she later, laughingly, confided in me that "I don't care where Rick is—we are not getting a cat!" Overall, this connection with Rick gave us an elated feeling of comfort and hope.

After Heidi and the kids decorated their Christmas tree, they hung up their stockings. It was very touching when six-year-old Calvin hung up a stocking for his dad and put a few gifts in it. One of the gifts he gave his dad was a pocket tool of some sort. It was times like these that were hard for me as a grandmother—seeing Calvin reach out to his dad with love and hope. He was so young. Trying to understand the mysteriousness of his missing dad was overwhelming. He was confused and hurt—he had been so close to Rick.

We all attended the Christmas Eve children's Mass at the local Catholic Church. It was nice because everyone from all sides of the families attended the same church. I always liked sitting together with my family at the services, but I also dreaded my crying when the music started at the time of communion. I just didn't want to draw attention but couldn't hold back the tears.

My oldest granddaughter, McKenzie, always came over by me and held my hand or just sat near me. This gave me such comfort.

There were times of laughter and fun, too. The whole family spent Christmas Eve at our house. The kids slept on the living room floor together and they had fun with the miniature flashlights and king-size chocolate bars that Tom and I gave them. I love all the commotion of a big family because that was the environment I grew up in. It's a comforting sound of security to me. There's nothing like hearing the laughter of kids playing while running through the house. This essence of family is what got me through the holidays.

There was one particular incident that deeply touched me during this time. Troy and Peggy's second son, Timmy, who was eight years old at the time, was asked at school what he wanted for Christmas. He was one of several kids that were interviewed. The questions and answers were printed in the local newspaper. I was surprised when I read what Timmy said, "I want my uncle Rick to be found so that my gramma Dolly will quit crying." It just warmed my heart that my eight-year-old grandson was so caring and that was his foremost thought. Most kids his age would have listed something material that they wanted for Christmas. I remember having a conversation with Timmy at the time. In an eight-year-old's mind he just couldn't understand that if someone was lost, why that person couldn't be found. Every one of my grandchildren during this time gave me loving support in their own special way.

My thoughts went back to about a year earlier during the holiday season. I was busy at work when Heidi called me late in the day and invited me to go to the movies with her, Rick, and the kids. I was flooded with work and didn't want to take the time off, but Heidi wouldn't take no for an answer and later I was glad that she was so insistent. The movie was just released and was titled *The Cat in the Hat*. We all thoroughly enjoyed that movie, laughing our heads off while eating popcorn. That will always be a happy memory for me, particularly because I distinctly remembered Rick's laughter.

Previous to this Christmas, Heidi and I had attended an annual memorial arranged by Hospice at the Lutheran Church. It was called "Celebration of Remembrance." We went directly to the chapel in the church. The lights were dimmed and there were candles burning on the altar. Though the atmosphere was one of sober thoughtfulness, I felt very comfortable and was thankful for this moment, at a time that was personally very special.

I prayed for the repose of Rick's soul. As I was kneeling and praying, I noticed other people around me and saw a couple on the other side of the church who had recently lost a fourteen-year-old son to cancer. My heart went out to them as I prayed for them and their son. After a while, Heidi and I went to the foyer where they were serving refreshments. Near a small Christmas tree on a table they offered specialized ornaments designed as praying hands. On one side of the ornament I had them write "Rick Hills" and on the other side "February 2004." There was a white ribbon attached so that I could hang it on my Christmas tree. Through tears, I had a conversation with the Hospice volunteer about attending grief classes, but never could bring myself to go through with it. It would have been good therapy, but at the time I was too grief stricken. I so appreciated this evening where I could commemorate Rick's passing.

Chapter Twenty-Four

Time was passing and we were now entering into another year, January 2005. Alaskan winters are cold and dark and can be very depressing. Dealing with the family's sad situation made it seem even worse. I worked long hours at my job, and though the conditions were very stressful, it enabled me to get through the day. Yet on the drive home I would have to release the suppressed grief I had held onto all day. I would literally be sobbing in my vehicle all the way home. I would try to get it all out before I reached my home so that I wouldn't distress Tom. As usual, being a typical man, he would try to fix it, not knowing how to handle emotion very well. On the other hand, I will always remember the one time I was crying and hurting so much I went into the garage where Tom was working. He just took me into his arms and held me. That was all I really needed or wanted. No words were necessary, just holding me was support enough.

Time felt like I was working my way through thick mud. My heart was so heavy it made my body feel like I was packing a ton of weight, though I only weighed a little over 100 pounds. Daily I forced myself to bundle up and go for a walk in the below-zero weather. I knew

I had to get out of the house for fresh air and exercise. Of course, I was continually praying and this gave me time to do that while I was alone.

Heidi was always thinking of me and concerned about my well-being. She made a prepaid appointment for a hot-rock massage for me. She strongly encouraged me to go, though I didn't feel up to it. I had known and was very comfortable with the lady who owned the spa and did the massage. Georgie was highly spiritual. She had an American Indian atmosphere in the cozy little massage room where the small bed had warm flannel sheets. I had her play Indian flute music, and with the lights dimmed down it quickly became very relaxing for me. Georgie always lays her hands on you and says a quiet prayer before beginning the massage. This is comforting. I became so relaxed I dozed while she was doing the massage and did not want to get up and get dressed to leave after the hour went by. Georgie knew I was deeply grieved and gave me a small black polished stone that was called an Apache Tear. She told me to rub it between my fingers anytime I felt I needed consoling or just to calm my emotions down. That was one of the best gifts I have ever received because I used that stone many, many times. I can't explain how it works nor do I care, but the energy from that stone really helped. I felt so much better after that hot-rock massage. It was like this heavy load was lifted off my shoulders. When I left the building and went outdoors it seemed like everything was so much better. I looked up toward the blue sky and thought to myself, "I'm going to make it. I'm going to live through this"! Thank you, God.

Chapter Twenty-Five

At this time my friend Karlene, who owned and operated Karlene's Acupunture and Day Spa, supported me by staying in close touch. We were like-minded in many ways and in the past she had helped both Tom and me with various physical issues. She phoned me one day to let me know that she had invited Kay, who was an intuitive, to her place of business. Kay had moved from England to Anchorage the previous year. Karlene knew that Kay, who was exceptionally gifted at making contact with loved ones that have passed, would be a huge relief and comfort to me. Some background on Kay may provide a better understanding about her role in my time of grief and how she greatly helped me.

As early as age three, Kay was aware of light forms and whispers. When she was five, her sister Karen, who had previously crossed over, visited regularly, sitting on the edge of her bed. Her presence allowed Kay to become comfortable with the many visitations that were to follow throughout her life. Her grandmother, an intuitive herself, helped Kay to understand why spirits were visiting— they were trying to teach and prepare her for her future.

Kay as a teenager had treated many injured animals. This intensified her communication and connection with the spirit world. She began receiving and giving messages, then healings, to anyone in need. In addition, her interest in all things spiritual took her around the world, from Mount Sinai to India and from England to Alaska.

I made an appointment for an hour reading with Kay. She knew very little about what happened to Rick except that he was missing. When we began the session the first message that came through from Rick was, "Mom, I'm okay." He felt he needed to explain the mystery of his disappearance—there were too many loose ends. Kay relayed seeing an image of a truck door being left open, Rick leaving in a hurry, having high anxiety. Someone was coming after him, which was a link to drugs and money involvement. Two angry guys were hot on his trail. (At this point Kay interjected that she felt Rick had passed on.)

Rick then further relayed that the guys who were after him did not take his life. As he kept on running, he was bleeding from an injury. He got lost and disoriented. He was in a dense, wooded area and eventually came to a standstill. Kay once again interjected that she felt I would not have any remains of Rick. (Speaking of this time period, she was correct.)

Rick continued that after he passed on he was relieved that the guys did not get to him. He died of exposure. He passed peacefully, though through trauma, and he knew it. A grandfather of strong Irish descent (my dad) came to take care of him. Rick was in a hospital environment and he was asleep on and off, taking a long time to recuperate. Kay relayed that Rick's primary concern was to give me comfort by tying up loose ends. He regretted falling in with the wrong group. He relayed, "Mom, I should have been stronger." He regretted putting me through all this and said, "Mom, you've been through hell and back." When I said, "I forgive you," Kay saw that Rick had tears in his eyes. Rick went on to say that he was helping people who took their own lives to pass over. He wanted to give something back. Kay said that Rick had contentment and peace of mind.

The reading went on further, but I need to share how important this session with Kay was to me. It was so personal and I truly felt Rick's presence and love. I felt such relief and had more peace of mind.

At a later visit to Soldotna from Anchorage, Kay stayed the night at Karlene's because we had previously planned to visit the area where Rick had disappeared and wanted to get an early start. When Heidi, Mack, and I showed up the next morning, Kay had something very interesting and extraordinary to tell us. She said that she had woken up in the middle of the night and that her head was *very* cold and the room temperature definitely felt below zero. She got up, turned up the thermostat in the room, and put on a snow cap and robe over her pajamas because it was so freezing cold in the room. She got back into bed and waited for the room to warm up but it never did. As she was lying there she said Rick appeared before her. He was standing there covered with frost with his arms slightly out to the side. She got the message that he wanted to show her that he was frosty. Kay could see trees behind Rick. Kay knew that Rick was attempting to show her that he had died of hypothermia. After Rick left, Kay said that the temperature in the room returned to normal.

We then got out the large, topical map that the Kenai Peninsula Borough had previously given to Tom. It was of the Sterling area where Rick had disappeared. We were looking for the spot where Rick had supposedly passed on. After Kay had studied the map she strongly felt we needed to check out a swamplike clearing that was located not too far from the road behind the airstrip where Rick was last known to be. Karlene's husband, Gary, had two snowmachines that we loaded up on a trailer. He towed these with his four-wheel-drive truck and drove to the area to search for the clearing. After arriving at the vicinity, we unloaded the snowmachines and started our search. We came upon a sort of clearing and were looking around. Kay and I both felt that this was not the place. We then rode the snowmachines back to where we first started and looked at the map again and decided that we needed to go directly into the woods from that spot to where we were pretty sure we would find the clearing we were looking for. It was right off the road and we followed a power line trail into the woods.

I have to say that I *really* felt we were going to find what we were searching for. It was as if I was being pushed. I ended up running and it wasn't easy. It was winter and we were all dressed up in cold-weather gear, included big snow boots. As the adrenaline ran through me I felt my heart racing like it was a hundred miles an hour. I was very excited for some unknown reason, other than that we were coming close to partially solving this mystery of Rick's disappearance.

As we came to this huge open clearing, I distinctly recalled a dream I'd had several days before Rick disappeared. I didn't quite understand it at the time.

> *Rick and I were floating as he had his right hand in mine.*
>
> *He was taking me to a place that felt very sad but peaceful.*
>
> *The setting was gray with light snowfall and it was wintertime.*
>
> *I could see what looked like a clearing amongst swamp spruce trees that surrounded the area.*

I had a melancholy feeling both during the dream and after I woke up. It was disturbing and seemed so real. I was so bonded with Rick that after putting two and two together, I wondered if I was receiving a message for what was to come.

We then continued into the clearing and came upon this tall spruce tree with a few smaller spruce trees near it. Kay strongly felt this was where Rick had died. I told Kay to try to connect with Rick and ask him if we were on the right spot. She said Rick was saying, "Mom, you are so close!" Kay could see an image of Rick, after running and getting tired, sliding down with his back up against a spruce tree in a clearing. Kay told me she could see Rick kissing me on my left cheek, which greatly warmed my being. We dug around in the snow looking for any evidence of Rick being there. It was difficult because the snow was so deep and it was tundra-like terrain. We circled the clearing going in opposite directions, hoping for a discovery of some kind. After quite a while we left and headed back to the road to the truck and snowmachines, only about a quarter of a mile away. It had been an exhausting morning but I was exhilarated because it seemed we were just a bit closer to understanding the obscure situation we were involved in.

I was up against a brick wall and had nothing more to go on but my intuition. I have discovered and learned, as I have been on this earth for some fifty-plus years that 99.99 percent of the time we should listen to our gut feelings. Nothing seems to go right if I don't follow that

"knowing". Sometimes you can't explain why you have to do the things you do, whether it is understood or not by others, but *you* know it is correct because of the powerful perception behind it. I do know to trust in God and pray for guidance each and every day and to always listen and trust that counsel of love given to me.

Kay also relayed to me that Rick was concerned with his family's well-being and peace of mind. He also said, "Mom, I know you. When you make up your mind about something, you pursue it." Because the circumstances involved drugs when Rick left this physical plane, he didn't want me to delve into the situation or ask too many questions. He was concerned for his family's safety with regard to the kind of people he had associated with. I appreciated this advice given through Kay, and chose to go cautiously with any investigating of my own, since it appeared that law enforcement was not moving forward in the case.

Kay also sought insight from an intuitive friend, Nancy, who lived in England. Kay told Nancy only two facts: Rick's first and last name and his birth date. She asked Nancy to relay any information stemming from that. Nancy said she saw someone that was very cold and still. There were lots of trees around but not in the middle of this area. She said, "This might seem odd, but I see someone up against a silver or white birch tree dying from exposure." I felt even more confident about Kay's information after hearing what Nancy had to say. I truly felt indebted to Kay because of the time she took away from home and family in Anchorage to travel to Soldotna to help find answers to Rick's disappearance. Kay would not accept any funds offered for her contribution of time involved. She genuinely was there to help. I finally began to slowly feel some closure which is what I had been praying so hard for.

> God, thank you for bringing people across my path to assist in this
>
> time of grieving. I fully trust in you, God, though I do not understand
>
> why we are all going through this very sad experience at this time in our lives.

I sincerely believe that there's a reason for everything. God closes one door only to open another. I have total faith in a Supreme Being.

Chapter Twenty-Six

In January 2005 Heidi received a long-distance phone call from a newspaper reporter, Tomas Tizan, who worked for the *Los Angeles Times*. His office was located in Seattle. He was interested in doing a story on missing people in Alaska and wanted to interview Heidi and me. We discussed the matter and decided a printed article would be a good opportunity for more public awareness regarding Rick's disappearance. After Heidi agreed to an interview, Tomas made arrangements fairly quickly to fly to Anchorage, rent a car, and drive down to the Kenai Peninsula. We agreed to meet in Sterling at a small restaurant. Tomas was a very warm and comfortable person to talk to, which made it easy for Heidi and me to totally open up to him.

During the interview we showed Tomas the large topical map of the area in Sterling in which Rick disappeared. Following the interview at the restaurant, we drove to the spot where Rick's truck was found and continued to drive throughout the subdivision. We showed Tomas the airstrip where Rick's tracks disappeared. At one point, we parked the car along the side of the road and walked a short distance to the riverbank that overlooked the Kenai River. It was a cold January day, but the sun was out and we were dressed for subzero weather. It felt good to walk and talk. It was therapeutic for me and I know Heidi felt the same. Overall, the long afternoon interview went very well, and when Heidi and I bid our new friend farewell we were the better for it. Tomas said he would shortly have a photographer contact us for pictures to go with the news article.

True to his word, a young man gave me a call not long afterwards and arranged to meet me at a local coffee shop in Soldotna. Jedediah was a photographer from the *Bristol Bay Times*, out of Dillingham, Alaska. This coincidentally was the village I was born in. I figured he'd take a few photos right there at the coffee shop and be on his way. But he suggested we go to my home and go from there. Tom and I actually visited with him quite awhile before he started taking pictures. I realized later that this was the purpose of the home visit, to get us in a comfortable and relaxed state, thus, better for picture taking. He took quite a few photos in front of our living room fireplace before moving us outdoors and shooting a bunch on our deck. It was a winter scene with our winter coats on and leafless trees in the background. Tom and I appear to be gazing off in the distance. One of these outdoor photos was chosen and it fit perfectly for the newspaper article. Jedediah did a very professional job and Tom and I were pleased with the outcome.

On February 15, 2005 I received an early-morning call from my friend, Janet, in Bakersfield. In an disbelieving tone, she said that she had seen the article regarding Rick's disappearance on the front page of the *Los Angeles Times*! She couldn't get over the fact that a picture and story from a small town in Soldotna, Alaska would show up in such an advertised and widespread newspaper. It was a very long article and also included other people missing from Alaska. The article was titled "Alaska, Land of the Lost" on the front page, and followed with "Vast Land Holds Secrets of the Missing" for the continuing story. The accompanying picture of Rick was my favorite. He was smiling as he held a trout he had just caught. The photo of Tom and me was somewhat larger and captured our solemn expression with both of us gazing off in different directions as in deep thought.

A few parts of the written article, when I reread them, always create a tug of pain in my heart. First, Dolly's words: "In my heart I know he's gone," she says. "I can feel it. Ricky and I were bonded. We were close. Ricky is not someone who disappears. Something happened to him." Here's what is written about the children: MacKenzie, 14, has come to believe her father is dead but can't say so. Katiebeth, 10, sees him in dreams that are hard to distinguish from the real world. The youngest, 6-year-old Calvin, continues to think that, like their dog Daisy that ran away, his dad went to do his own thing for a while and soon will return. Heidi said, "Up till now I don't have anything to say, Look, this is what happened to your dad."

Tomas Tizon said that most of the time, the one prominent newspaper in Anchorage, a widely read paper in the state, picks up his stories. I waited for several weeks and when I didn't see his story printed I called the chief editor of this paper and inquired why they hadn't printed Tomas Tizon's article about missing persons in Alaska. I talked to several persons in charge to get an answer. I was told this was an article that they just decided not to print. I strongly urged them to reconsider because they might possibly be able to help find some of the missing people involved. Some of them were very young. I told them that I believed that my own son was gone but here was an opportunity to perhaps help find others that may still be alive. I was politely rebuffed. I was very disappointed, though this article was picked up by many newspapers throughout the United States. For example, I had copies sent to me from people that picked up the article in newspapers from Minnesota and Honolulu.

Tomas Tizon said that he had even received a call from a movie producer in New York who was interested in making a movie about Rick, but nothing came of it.

Chapter Twenty-Seven

On February 4, 2005 we had a presumptive death hearing at the Kenai Court House. It's common to wait for about a year before a presumptive death hearing can take place on a missing person. I knew this hearing would be very hard on Heidi and me emotionally because we would be summoned. Larry, the State Trooper was also summoned as a witness. I told Tom about this hearing but he didn't fully realize what was taking place and I didn't push him to be there because he would have been uncomfortable in this type of atmosphere. I knew it would be better for me to handle it without him. Peggy, my daughter-in-law, attended. I was appreciative of that because I really felt support with her presence. Cindi, Heidi's mother, had flown up from the States and I was so grateful she was able to be there for Heidi. Quite a few of Heidi's friends also attended, which was thoughtful and good support.

Before the hearing the judge took Heidi and me back to his chambers for a briefing on what would take place. I'll never forget the kindness and compassion that his man showed. He stated that he wanted to make this hearing go as quickly and easily as possible for us, because he understood the painful emotions we would be processing at a time like this. I had the Apache Tear stone with me. It really helped me when it was my turn to witness. I would rub the stone with my right thumb and forefinger. This helped me to keep my emotions in check when I had to speak. I still had a shaky, tearful voice but was able to answer all the questions the judge asked. Heidi did well speaking. It was ironic that she was emotional before the hearing and I wasn't. During the hearing it was vice versa. Larry presented his report in a very professional manner considering the sensitive nature of the subject.

During the hearing I couldn't help recall being in that same courtroom several years earlier when Rick was on trial for a misdemeanor. As he was waiting in the courtroom to be presented before the judge, I was in the audience seated, holding my rosary. When Rick and I made eye contact I quickly held up my prayer beads to show support. That brought on a typical "Ricky grin" in return, and at the same time, a feeling of love and understanding between mother and son.

In conclusion, the summary of evidence for death read as follows: "Richard T. Hills, after consuming alcohol and controlled substances, lost control of a vehicle he was driving. He abandoned the vehicle, became disoriented and wandered off into the woods and wilderness area adjacent to the Kenai River and the Kenai Keys subdivision area of Sterling, Alaska. Due to the level of intoxication, Mr. Hills succumbed to hypothermia and/or drowning." Heidi and I were very relieved when this hearing was completed, as the family so badly needed some type of closure, especially the children. It was something "to go on" for an answer, instead of a big question mark regarding their dad. For me it helped finalize that Rick was officially "gone." (I never did like that word *dead*. When I was a kid I always referred to death as "kicking the bucket," a saying I picked up from my dad.)

The whole day had been an emotional process and therefore exhausting. Now that the presumptive death hearing was done, the next event to follow would be the funeral service. We wanted to do that as soon as possible, especially for the children's sakes. We decided the memorial would be held at 2 p.m. Saturday at Our Lady of Perpetual Help, the Catholic Church in Soldotna. This gave us a little more than a week for preparations. We immediately phoned close friends and family the evening of the presumptive death hearing to notify them of the time, as some were out of state. Some relatives were very unhappy with the date set for the memorial service because it didn't fit into their schedule to attend, since they were out of town. Heidi and I both had to deal with this via phone and it was unfortunate because we were already down and out after going through the emotions of the death hearing earlier in the day. I tried to be as positive as possible about the situation, but it did put more of a damper on things. I very much wanted to move forward with the memorial service as soon as possible, because after nearly a year of *not* knowing we all badly needed closure, especially the children! As far as I was concerned, Rick's immediate family (Heidi and the kids) were the priority.

Chapter Twenty-Eight

R ick's obituary came out on February 8, 2005. Some of what was written in the article so that you can familiarize yourself with Rick:

> Mr. Hills was born June 4, 1968, in Soldotna to Tom and Dolly Hills. He graduated from Soldotna High School in 1987 and worked in the oilfields on the North Slope and on offshore platforms. He spent many summers commercial fishing in Bristol Bay and Cook Inlet. Rick loved spending time with his family, especially if they went fishing with him. Rick enjoyed cooking, fishing, hockey, snowmachining, and staying busy. Rick also cherished times spent with his dear friends Jack Wright, Joe Schultz and best friend Kurt Saltenberger. Rick was very charming and had a great sense of humor and a contagious smile. He was very respectful of his elders and was always willing to help anyone who needed help. He was a hard worker and was always at peace while fishing on the river. "We will miss Rick dearly, but he will forever be in our hearts," his family said.

It was a cold, windy, wintry day during the time of the memorial service. In the foyer of the church we had several pictures displaying Rick, family, and friends. I particularly liked one huge framed photo of Rick and Kurt Saltenberger. It was taken right after they graduated from high school. They both had big smiles on their faces and it was a great reminder of happier times. When Kurt came into the foyer to attend the service, he took one look at that photo and had to turn and leave with tears in his eyes. This was very hard on Kurt since he and Rick were very close. I had asked him previously to speak at the service, but he wasn't sure if he'd be able. I encouraged him to do so—even up to the last minute.

Little Calvin looked so nice in his white shirt, black tie, and slacks. My heart went out to him so much because even before the service began he was very emotional. I can only imagine what was going through his six-year-old mind, trying to absorb what this memorial service represented, that his dad was gone and was not going to come back. This reality had to be very painful to face. I told everyone that we had to get the service started because I didn't want it to be any more drawn out than necessary, especially for the sake of the children.

Tom and I sat in the left front row of the church. I had brought a washcloth because I knew I'd be crying a lot and I didn't want umpteen pieces of tissues on my lap. Also, I could muffle my emotions somewhat. During the service I looked over at Rosie and she was looking at me laughing because of that washcloth up to my face.

I couldn't help but smile to myself because she had such a sense of humor—like my side of the family—even at a sad time like this. It warmed my heart somewhat. Six-year-old Calvin, on the other hand, had a very hard time. He was sitting next to me and was literally sobbing with his head down on his arm leaning against the front pew. I wished there was some way I could take his pain away no matter how much I was already hurting. I think all parents and grandparents would feel the same way in this situation.

Father Tero did a very appropriate and short homily. He talked about Rick's disappearance and said this was a mystery in God's hands, and when we see the Lord this mystery will be revealed to us.

I was relieved when Kurt Saltenberger got up to speak. He did it so well. He mentioned that Rick always talked about commercial fishing with his uncle Ray and how much he had learned through those experiences each summer. He said Rick had good work ethics he had learned through his dad, and a good sense of humor from his Mom.

Another friend of Rick's, Joe Schultz, also spoke. With his quiet demeanor, I know it wasn't easy for Joe to stand before an audience to perform that task, but he spoke from the heart and I really appreciated his talk.

Tom got up at the last minute to say a few words, which I thought was very brave, because I surely couldn't. I was too distraught. One of the things that Tom said that brought a bit of laughter was that "Rick was always willing to give a helping hand—he might not show up on time but he would show up!" This brought on a quiet laughter from the audience.

At the end of the service I had requested that the country western song by George Strait, "It's a Love Without End, Amen" be played. I love the lyrics to that song, especially these lines:

Let me tell you a secret about a father's love,

you see, daddies don't just love their children every now and then.

It's a love without end, amen.

Last night I dreamed I died and stood outside those pearly gates.

When suddenly I realized there must be some mistake.

If they know half the things I've done, they'll never let me in.

And then somewhere from the other side I heard these words again:

"Let me tell you a secret about a father's love, it's a love without end, amen."

I chose this song because it was so Rick.

We had received so many beautiful bouquets. My favorite one was the one Janet Rickard sent from California. It was an arrangement with a big cross surrounded by flowers. I also had been given plants that I still have today.

After the service we had a get-together at our house. We were all so emotionally drained and relieved that the memorial service had finally taken place. Now perhaps this would help all of us gradually *let go* and keep moving forward, no matter how slowly for some of us. I was one of those who had a very hard time letting go, though at the time I didn't realize that. I was doing all the right things outwardly to heal, but Rick was so locked into my being that I felt I was really taking tiny baby steps to move on. It was like I was trying to push a brick wall in front of me so that I could trek down that long trail that was ahead of me. I knew it would take a long time and wished I could skip ahead of time, but I had enough faith to know that God was very patient and loving and that He would help me all the way, no matter how long I took.

Heidi put a nice message in the next issue of the local newspaper following the memorial service. She included a picture of Rick, which was my favorite because of his huge, happy smile:

> The family of RICK HILLS would like to thank our many friends and family members who have given their support and prayers or have sent flowers. We thank you all for being here for us this past year, since Rick's disappearance. We are truly blessed to have you in our lives.

The next morning we got up fairly early. Tom fixed breakfast for our guests, who had a three-hour drive ahead of them back to Anchorage. After eating very little, and with our guests gone, I lay down on the couch and was there most of the day. I felt I had no strength in me, and try as I might, I could not move from where I was. I knew I had to try to start eating so I would at least feel better physically. Besides, I still had a job I had to go to, like everybody else. Somehow, I knew I would persevere. It would take time, whether I liked it or not. Everyone else in the family was in the same boat. I felt so fortunate to be surrounded by such caring loved ones who gave support to each other, each in his or her own way.

An article I had read from Hospice described grief and mourning in a very fitting manner:

> Grief is a natural expression of love. A reaction to a change in our lives—to loss.
>
> It is usually initially emotional, not intellectual—it occurs within us.
>
> It is a mixture of emotions.
>
> It is the most painful form of loneliness— that which comes with the loss of a loved one —life will never be the same.
>
> Mourning is grief gone public, taking the grief within us and sharing it outside of ourselves. It is hard to heal without mourning.
>
> There is no right or wrong way to grieve and each individual will grieve and mourn in their way.
>
> Grief is not something to "get over". It is possible to reconcile grief—to go on with life— but it's not something that will be forgotten. There is no time limit to grieving.

Chapter Twenty-Nine

The following describes an adventurous and exciting event that helped Tom so much to cope with the loss of Rick.

In the middle of March, the annual winter king fishing derby took place in Homer, Alaska. As a dedicated sportfisherman, Tom was excited and looked forward to this big event. Additionally, it would be a nice reprieve from the solemn atmosphere of home. I felt relief and happiness for Tom as he busily prepared his 22-foot Hewescraft Sea Runner hardtop boat for this widely advertised and popular fishing contest.

Two of his fishing buddies would be going with him. They left Soldotna in the early morning hours for the ninety-minute drive to Homer for the all-day event. About three hundred boats entered the fishing derby. It was a very crisp and cold day with ice still in the water, but Tom had a good heater in the cabin of the boat. It took about an hour to travel to the preplanned fishing spot.

They had been fishing only about an hour when Tom all of a sudden hooked into a good-sized feeder king! Emotions were running high because they all knew it could possibly be a winner. They put the fish into an aluminum container with water just covering it. This would avoid shrinkage and keep it at the heaviest weight possible for the documented weighing when they got back into Homer later. Without delay Tom called in to report the fish to the Homer Chamber of Commerce headquarters who were putting on the contest.

For the rest of the afternoon no one else in their boat caught or hooked into anything of real size. At the end of the day when they returned to Homer, Tom had a really nice picture taken, holding his prize fish. Posing, he had the nicest and biggest grin ever! Tom's feeder king weighed in at thirty-two pounds and came in second place. Needless to say, all three guys were ecstatic. Along with the prize money and the extra side bets that had been placed, they had won over twenty thousand dollars. They split it three ways. It had been a fun and memorable day. Tom had no problem sleeping that night! I thanked God for bringing them all safely home and bringing that gift of joy to Tom. He needed the extra lift at this time of challenge in his life.

Chapter Thirty

E arly spring of 2005, the fishing derby complete, brought our family back to Rick's passing.

Heidi received a long-distance phone call from a movie production studio, Planet Grande Pictures, located in Malibu, California. After reading the *Los Angeles Times* article about Rick, titled "Alaska, Land of the Lost," they were interested in filming the story on the TV program called *CMT Small Town Secrets*. Heidi contacted me to see what my thoughts and feelings were about the offer. I agreed with her that we should do it because just maybe, after the story was aired on national TV, we could get some unsolved answers from local viewers.

Heidi agreed to the studio's offer and arrangements were made for a TV crew of four to fly up from California. When Heidi and I met with them at the coffee shop where Heidi worked, we reviewed all the details of the making of the film, including who would be the participants. On the morning of the planned filming, the crew, in their own vehicle, followed Heidi, Tom, Kurt, Kay, and me out to the Sterling area to the spot where Rick's abandoned truck was found. We started from there to begin the story.

Tom did such an excellent job of recalling all the events in the right order and verbalizing his feelings. In a nutshell, he stated that he did not want to think that Rick disappeared because of foul play, because he did not want to hate. Tom said, "I have no feelings, I don't try to guess, I just know that Rick disappeared. You can pick the end you choose. Hypothermia is a good way to go. You get tired, warm, sleepy, and it's over and it's peaceful."

For my part I implored anyone having any information on Rick's disappearance to please come forward. It was *so* important to the family, I said. I went on to say, "I am a forgiving person," referring to the possibility that foul play was involved.

Heidi recalled that she knew something serious happened when the State Troopers came to her door to inform her that a truck registered under her name was found in a ditch. She said Rick "always called, always came home." Kurt gave a good message about substance abuse. He commented, "We are a small town, the drugs that have hit the bigger cities are now hitting this town! The meth is really destroying a lot of families." Kay relayed that the information she received from Rick was of concern for his family. She said that when we pass on we still have the same feelings as when we were alive. Regarding Rick's disappearance, Kay further relayed that she was shown a clearing.

State Trooper Lt. McDonald was also included in the story and his input was done in a very professional manner. He stated that substances were found in the vehicle which gave indication that Rick was impaired, that he didn't know what happened to Rick—he could have gotten lost in the woods or wandered into the river.

Overall, I was very pleased the way the film turned out. We received a copy of it in the mail, and after watching it, I called the Planet Grande Pictures office and gave my heartfelt thanks to them for doing such a good job on their production.

When we watched the film for the first time as a family, it was very difficult and I became very emotional. I was so grateful for my oldest granddaughter, Mack, who sat with me and held my hand. Words don't necessarily need to be spoken at times like this, but touch can give you such a sense of love and well-being.

After this film was shown many times on national TV, a lot of acquaintances over the years informed Tom and me that, until viewing this story on *CMT Small Town Secrets*, they hadn't even realized that we had a son missing.

Seeing this film together as family was good therapy for all involved, especially Tom. Originally, he had not planned to participate, but I'm so glad he changed his mind. He made it come together because he did so well in explaining the time line of events. Also, it gave him an opportunity to express how he felt. He may not have realized it, but by openly verbalizing his feelings, he released some tension held within. When I look back on it, I see God holding our hands and gently leading us all forward. We as a family were learning patience whether we liked it or not. Because I especially have always been very impatient, this was one time when I had no control over how quickly the answers we all

so desperately needed and wanted would be revealed.
Chapter Thirty-One

In retrospect, I felt that all through these events, the situation was painfully inching forward. I was still distressed, because even though Heidi and I often made visits to the State Troopers, we were not getting any new information or answers. When I arranged meetings, I often felt we were just a pain in the butt. Most of the investigators and officers were attentive and did what they could to help, but as time passed and new people replaced the old, it seemed by the disinterested manner I sensed, that the case was turning cold. Heidi and I did a lot of investigating on our own. We talked to many people who gave us bits and pieces of information, but not enough to close the gap, so to speak. Nevertheless, it made us feel like we were trying and in return it gave us some consolation. Any new bit of knowledge or fact we acquired was passed on to the authorities. But then again, if we could not provide proof, the information was useless.

It just so happened that Tom and I were struggling with finances at this same time. This was the first time in our lives that we were so financially challenged. We have had hard times before, just like a lot of people, but this time we were just about at the end of our rope concerning money matters. Strictly speaking, we were struggling to avoid bankruptcy. I was determined not to let this happen and absolutely would not give in to the idea. It went against everything in my being. So, along with praying constantly regarding Rick, I intently prayed for financial stability. Every spare moment during my waking hours was used in fervent communication with the Almighty, stating that I refused to go down that road and that I desperately needed His help and guidance in our current financial situation. God is limitless in His power, so I always ended my conversations with, "Thy will be done." He does see the big picture.

Simultaneously I was going through some health changes which was more of an irritation than anything, and it made me feel frustrated on top of everything else. It seemed like I was constantly trying to find some balance in the middle of everything. Prayer was the one and only thing that really kept me somewhat steadfast. Through manifestation, I could see the light at the end of the tunnel, but I knew it was still going to be a continuing struggle before that time came. I often wished I could skip ahead from point A to point B in time to avoid all the suffering in between, but I believed God's plan for me and my family was in perfect order. I could not rush His perfect timing, but just believed that everything in my topsy-turvy life would eventually get ironed out. I had to have a healthy and positive outlook in order to heal in all areas of my life.

With all this turmoil and with so much on my mind, it was no wonder that I had a vehicle mishap on my way to work. It was a crispy April morning around seven. Thank goodness I wasn't yet to the highway when I heard this knocking sound coming from my engine. I couldn't figure out what the heck it was. So I pulled over to the side of the road and called Tom from my cell and explained the noise to him. He knew immediately what it was. He asked me what my oil gauge registered at. The needle looked below the low level! I couldn't believe I had let the oil run out. I had always been very prompt on checking it and I had completely forgotten about it. Sure enough, when Tom checked it out further, he told me that the engine had blown up! Even this didn't really phase me at the time. It seemed such a trivial thing compared to everything else that was on my mind. So I sold the vehicle dirt cheap and purchased another. I think I came out ahead in the long run because the newer car I bought had better gas mileage.

Material things at this time of my life didn't mean a hill of beans to me. I was completely indifferent to such things. As a matter of fact, I was telling my son Troy that if I drove up to my house and it was nothing but a pile of ash, it would not matter to me. He couldn't understand that until he got to thinking about how he'd feel if anything happened to one of his children. Then he could relate to my state of mind. I was sure that one day all this would pass, but at the time it seemed like it would be a long way off.

On Mother's Day 2005 I was distraught as usual and trying to keep my "sense of being" together. After coming home from work that evening I decided to bake some pies to keep busy. Tom said that up to this time of his life he had never seen so many pies baked! It always took me some time because I made my own crust and filling. I was hurting so much that I was literally running about my kitchen preparing these pies. While I was mixing the filling for one of the pies, I was praying very hard for Rick to just give me some sort of sign that he was around. I felt this reassurance would give me a lot of comfort. Then for no reason, all of a sudden I just put down the mixer and walked directly to my bedroom and went over to my dresser. A card that Rick had given me which I kept on the left side of my dresser was face down on the opposite end! There was no breeze in the room because no window was open and no fan was going. A very strong *knowing* came over me and I distinctly knew that Rick had answered my request. I felt so elated. I thanked God for this communication with my son. This was very personal and beyond words to explain. It was a true experience and the best Mother's Day gift I could ever have asked for.

Chapter Thirty-Two

My grandchildren were a great support to me, each in his or her own special way. Mack was always there to hold my hand when she would see that I was emotionally stressed. Many times in church she would slip in beside me to hold my hand in comfort when she noticed me crying. Craig knew I was hurting. A lot of times Craig was present while I was distressfully venting to Peg. With his quiet way and the kind look in his eyes, I could feel his compassion, though he may not always have understood what I was discussing. Rosie always had a big smile and giggle to distract me from my sadness, and my spirits would lift—even momentarily this helped. When she really laughed, it was deep down from her belly and it just tickled everybody. Timmy was very thoughtful. At one time he brought a rather large round stone to me. He had printed on its sandy-colored surface with a black marker, "We love you, Rick". His thoughtfulness, at such a young age, really warmed me. I kept that stone until the message faded. Calvin, with his pain at losing the dad that he was so close to, had an understanding connection. He always said, after watching the CMT story regarding his dad, "That is sooo sad." Danielle was so young at the time she did not know what was really going on. I always liked her around because she had a comforting presence in all her innocence. I enjoyed her company even if she was quietly coloring or humming. Those big brown eyes and warm smile were always a joy to see. Children are such a blessing in disguise. Just hearing them laughing, chatting, or playing gets you out of yourself and brings light, creating a warm and positive atmosphere.

My grandchildren were really the loved ones that kept me going. I knew if nothing else, I had to be there for each and every one of them. They were there (unknowingly) for me! I constantly thank God for this special gift of grandchildren which He has given Tom and me. They all have unique personalities and that's what I really enjoy. It's never boring having our grandchildren around.

Mack, Rosie, and Calvin spent the summer of 2005 in the Lower 48 states visiting relatives, while Heidi stayed here and kept very busy in self-employment.

I was really tied up with work. Summers in Alaska boom. We have a short three months and everything is crammed into that time frame—tourists, construction, and so forth.

Despite a certain normalcy returning to the family I felt unsettled. Several times during the summer I had gone to the site in Sterling where Rick had disappeared. I was trying to find some sort of peace of mind, not really knowing what I was searching or looking for. I was so lost . . . trying to keep my sanity.

I also made visits to two different rehab organizations that summer. I shared with participants the DVD from

Small Town Secrets regarding Rick, and offered to speak to any interested parties. My aim was to encourage the clients to move forward in their recovery from substance abuse by telling them my story. I was invited to attend a meeting at a facility Rick had previously considered going to. It was located on the banks of the Kenai River and it had a serene atmosphere. I was emotional at times, but overall the talk went very well. The group was small and very attentive and I answered questions afterwards. It made me feel better to give that talk. To put it plainly, I believe that I wanted to make something good out of something bad that happened. Would it make a difference to any one of these people if they could hear a distraught mother speak about losing her son because of substance abuse?! I wondered ... I hoped ... I prayed. I cared for every one of those clients, and I gave them full credit for trying to make changes for the better in their lives.

In August 2005, our younger son, Troy, found promising work in Colorado Springs, Colorado. He left Alaska ahead of his wife, Peggy, and the kids, to get established in his new job and look for a place to live. The family followed in October. This was a positive decision for them. A change for the better!

By the end of October I was no longer working and this was a good thing. I was run down mentally and physically and I felt like I could just drop! That's exactly what it seemed like I did. When I got up in the morning I put my big, fuzzy robe on and went directly to the living room with my cup of coffee and proceeded to build 500- and 1,000-piece puzzles, with the TV turned on to a western movie. I did this routinely for several hours in the morning for about a month. Tom was beginning to wonder about this, since it isn't in my character to be so lax and sluggish.

Neither Tom nor anyone else at the time really understood what I was feeling. It was almost like I collapsed and was doing what I needed to do to mend myself. I was totally shutting out everything that was stressful and at the same time keeping occupied with something that I enjoyed doing. Building those jigsaw puzzles kept my mind busy. I just wanted to be by myself and do my own thing, until I could start feeling better. I believe that God gave me direction intuitively so that I could help myself. After about a month of this, I was better. I felt like I could function a little more normally again.

Chapter Thirty-Three

I n December '05 Tom received a petit jury summons for January jury duty. The following is a letter he addressed to the court dated 15-15-05.

Your Honor,

I wish to be excused permanently from jury duty. In the past I have served a couple of different times on a Grand Jury, but don't feel I could be completely objective due to recent events.

In February of 2004 my son, Richard Thomas Hills, disappeared on Kenai Keys Road. He was 35 years old. In February of this year we had a presumptive death hearing because his body was never found. We know from rumors & bits of evidence that the whole thing was drug related and foul play was involved.

I couldn't be fair dealing in any case involving drug or violence.

Thanx
Tom Hills

Since Tom tends to keep his thoughts to himself I liked the way he expressed his feelings in explaining Rick's disappearance to the judge. It gave me some insight to what he honestly felt.

On 23 December 2005 the court clerk verified that the letter had been received and had been passed on to Judge Landry, the same judge who had presided over Rick's presumptive death hearing. On December 29 of that year we received a notice that Tom had been excused from jury duty. Both Tom and I appreciated the court's respect and understanding in handling the situation.

Shortly after Christmas Tom and I took a short but much-needed vacation. We were invited to go on a cruise through the Gulf of Mexico with some friends who were celebrating the fiftieth wedding anniversary of their parents. There were about fifty people in the group. Tom and I flew into Dallas, Texas and rented a car. We had flown out a few days before the cruise departure date so that we could have time to tour part of Texas. I love history, so it was fun and interesting to drive southwest down towards San Antonio, stopping at different historical sites. At Corpus Christi we drove east toward Galveston along the picturesque coastline. We reunited with the group of travelers and stayed one night at a hotel in Galveston before departing on our cruise to Mexico.

This was just what Tom and I needed mentally—to relax and be among friends celebrating a happy occasion. It was nice to have a short reprieve from the cold winter of Alaska and be in some sunshine. This especially did

Tom a world of good. We both temporarily left the reminders of stress behind and enjoyed the moment in time.

Because of storms, we had to bypass a couple of scheduled tourist spots. But at Cosumel we thoroughly enjoyed an area where we waded in very shallow water with stingrays swimming about. A guide even had one slither up my back, a most interesting experience. The water was a clear blue with a sandy white bottom. It was warm, soothing, and calming. What a beautiful sunny day!

Visiting Jamaica was somewhat disturbing because of the poverty. As we disembarked the ship, a group of children, dressed in shabby white uniforms, played in the band, under the hot sun. You wondered just how much of the money they individually received from the donation bucket that was passed around to their audience. It was a reminder to be very grateful for the country we were born in and the opportunities that are available compared to what these poor people had. The scene of this impoverished country will forever stay in my mind. I am glad for that, because it's a reminder to me to always keep less fortunate people in my prayers.

The cruise lasted for only about a week, but it was long enough for Tom and me to feel refreshed at the end of the journey. It was especially pleasant for Tom, since it was his first cruise.

Reluctantly, we returned to another seemingly long, cold, and snowy winter in Alaska. I was grateful for having Heidi and the kids around, since Troy's family had moved out of state. Twelve-year-old Rosie wrote a note for Tom and me dated 2-12-06. It warmed our hearts. I will copy it just as she wrote it. (Take note: the grandkids always referred to Tom as "grumpa". This was started by then six-year-old Calvin.)

> *Dear grandma and grumpa,*
>
> *you have done so much for us and now we are catching up slowly. you are one of the specil people in our lives. We love you so much.*
>
> *from: The kids who drive you to drink!*
>
> *We love you both .with all of our harts!*
>
> *Heidi and family*
>
> *Rosie Rote this leter.*

This letter was both comical and touching. Our grandchildren were a real reminder to keep us moving forward. Whether we realized it at the time or not, they were very consoling in their own innocent and carefree ways.

Chapter Thirty-Four

Another winter went by and the second anniversary of Rick's passing in late February was processed once again. Though it had been two years since Rick had been gone, it seemed like just yesterday. The wounds still ran deep within me and I so wanted this wound to heal, though I knew that scars would remain. I wanted to jump ahead of time when the deep pain would be only skin deep. For me, I felt that so far in life, this was the greatest physical, emotional, and spiritual challenge I had come up against. Since I am a confronter, this experience was the most difficult to face head-on. I did everything I could think of to help myself to move on. I made a physical effort to walk (many miles a day), talk (to anyone available), and pray (constantly). I thought of my mother, who had a saying that always popped up in my mind: "In time the wound heals." It just seemed like it was taking so damned long! But I also understood realistically that pain always does. This is where I was practicing patience whether I liked it or not.

I had to keep busy and I loved working mornings the best. That was the time I had the most energy. I went to work part time for Karlene's Acupuncture and Day Spa in July of that summer. The hours were perfect, because I worked form 8:30 a.m. to 12:30 p.m. most of the time. It was only five minutes' driving time from my house. I truly enjoyed working as a jack of all trades at this place of business. I was a receptionist and bookkeeping assistant, ran errands, changed sheets for the acupuncture and massage clients, prepared the spa clients for services, and sold and stocked vitamins, herbs, and spa supplies. It also had an atmosphere of spirituality. The appealing aroma when you entered the building was a combination of incense, massage oils, and candles. It was very inviting. The services she offered helped many clients. It was very satisfying and exciting for me to be a part of this.

Every morning I would go to work a little early and go to a back room where meetings were held. It had a small kitchenette area with a divider and a dim light to one side. One wall had a dome surrounding a large mural that covered the inside wall. It was a scene of a waterfall and small river with lots of colorful trees with blossoms. For me this was a very inviting atmosphere to do a few minutes of meditation before starting my day.

I also did a lot of mental communicating with Rick. I pictured him in a very peaceful and loving place with water similar to the scene of the mural. Doing this ritual every working morning helped me immensely to be more centered throughout the day. I truly felt God's peace and love. It was no mistake that I was working in this place of healing. God puts each one of us where we need to be when we seek His guidance.

Karlene also knew Kay. She offered her facility as a meeting place for Kay to give readings to her clients.

It was an opportunity for me to receive readings through Kay. This helped me immensely as I received more information from Rick regarding the mystery of his disappearance. Little by little I felt more consoled and more at peace. These readings were so personal between me and my son. His presence was close as ever to me. The only difference was that I was learning to make the adjustment to communicate with him in the spiritual, just as if he was here in the physical. Rick conveyed that we only need to think of him or call on him and he would be with us instantly through thought. This was a solace for me.

In October '06 Tom wanted to get me a Boston terrier dog for my birthday. We've previously owned this type of breed on more than one occasion and thoroughly enjoyed them. We couldn't find one locally and looked in the advertisements of the Anchorage paper. There was one for sale for half price which was good news because they are expensive dogs. Tom called the owner, who was a breeder and found out that the female dog wasn't able to carry pups, so they needed to sell her. I was pretty happy as I had wanted a female. I had also been praying that if this was the dog we were to own in the future, everything would work out for purchasing her.

We drove the 150 fifty miles to Anchorage to visit with the owner and the dog. Tom and I fell in love with her. She was very small and looked somewhat undernourished. We excitedly bought her on the spot. I already had the name picked out which would be Rikki. This would be good therapy for me and the family, especially the grandkids. Sometimes it's hard for family to mention the name of a loved one who has passed on. I thought this would be good practice for all of us and it would be something tangible that we could embrace and love. There's something soothing about holding and petting an animal. This was very healing for all of us, as Rikki enjoyed being loved and held. We took her to a vet and had some bad teeth pulled, updated her shots, and got her on some nutritious dog food. In no time at all Rikki fattened up and had a very glossy coat. Within a month she looked so much healthier that I believe she could have carried pups—if we so desired. Because she had been raised in a kennel she hadn't been taught or nurtured as a pet. We had her for a month before we ever heard her bark. Rikki had to be taught to chew on bones and play. She and I thoroughly enjoyed our many walks together and the grandkids loved her. It was no coincidence that we got this very lovable animal.

Chapter Thirty-Five

Peggy, my daughter-in-law, was now living in Colorado Springs with Troy and their children. She worked long-distance by phone with the City of Kenai to purchase a 9-by-12 memorial stone plaque for Rick. This would be displayed at the Lief Hansen Memorial Park located in the center of Kenai. This park is beautifully landscaped and especially appealing in summer when the grass is fully green and trees in full bloom. This would be a gift for Rosie and Calvin in memory of their dad. We all worked together to choose the most appropriate carving and inscription on the stone. At the top of the stone are inscribed the words: REMEMBERING A FATHER'S LOVE. Below there is a carved picture of a young man, with a fishing pole in hand, standing on a riverbank fishing. The sun is peacefully reflected on the water. Ironically, the young man very much resembled Rick. He is standing and wearing a cap like Rick always did. Below the scene are the words: RICK HILLS 1968–2004. I appreciated that thoughtful gesture of Peg. Tom and I often go there to reflect. There's a sense of peace with each visit.

Yet, in the family as a whole, reconciliation was a long process. One day as I was leaving my house and driving down the road toward the highway, I got a call on my cell from Heidi. This was several years after Rick passed away. She was a bit agitated and wanted to share her thoughts and feelings with me. Heidi and I had always done this. It was comforting because we understood and trusted each other.

On that day, she was venting about her disappointment in the State Troopers for not "getting anywhere with Rick's case." As I listened with a sympathetic ear, I literally felt, in a physical sense, my body partially letting go of Rick! This is an experience I will always recall because it was such an enlightening moment. It was a release of energy that emerged from the torso of my body, as in the center chakra or heart area. I could tell it was only a partial surrender, but I felt immediately so much lighter and free from the emotional pain.

I will never forget that relinquishing experience. Through this personal encounter, I realized that even though I had *accepted* Rick's death, I hadn't *let go* of Rick. For me, I learned that *accepting* and *letting go* of death are two different experiences. It was such a relief of body, mind, and soul. I felt so much better. In time, I gradually let go of Rick completely. I have always known it's healthy to let go of someone who has passed and not to hang on for a prolonged period of time, but I found it is easier said than done. I believe everyone handles this in a different way when the time comes. Since losing a child was a new experience for me, it was as if I was going through a spiritual learning process, though I may not have known it at the time. As I write this

I am still learning and continually practicing—for my own benefit—to turn everything over to God, no matter how small the situation or problem may seem. Maybe it's partially my age and a diminishing of my ego, along with practice, that I willingly always try to let go. For me, it takes honest prayer, which in turn gives me comfort.

In January 2009, when Rosie was fourteen years old, she wrote a paper about her dad for a class assignment in school. This was very touching and I would like to share it with you:

> *The person that has changed my life most would be my dad. He was a nice loving family guy; he cared most about his family. He'd do anything for anybody. He had the friendliest personality you could ever imagine, very warm hearted.*
>
> *When I was little I never realized any of that about him. I never took the time to get along and realize he really was a great dad to me. He would always try so hard, do the best he could, and gave it his all. I really looked up to him for always doing the hard work he did.*
>
> *He would cheer me up the times we would hang out together; he'd take me fishing, or offer to get me something. Every night he would go down to the bridge and me, him or him and my brother would always catch the nice sized silvers.*
>
> *He was always so happy and nice, no matter what. If we got in trouble he would still be happy with us and not mad. He was easy going and*

always forgot about it. When I was down he would always be there and try to cheer me up. He never liked to see his kids that way.

Now that he is gone I really notice all what he did for me. Also how he was always there, always positive, always had the biggest smile on his face. I loved that most about him. He made the biggest change in my life ever. I don't think anybody else could ever change it as much as he did.

This was such a tribute to Rick from the heart of his daughter. Rosie has always appeared to have a spiritual sensitivity. She shared another moving experience with me in April 2010, when she was fifteen. She was listening to a song at 7 a.m. while in the bathroom, getting ready for school. The song was "It Won't Be Like This for Long" by Darius Rucker. She said the song stopped and then repeated the part that said, "He lays down there beside her 'Til her eyes were finally closed, and just watching her breaks his heart 'cause he already knows, it won't be like this for long." Through this Rosie felt a communication with her dad. It was always comfortable for Rosie to share her experiences and thoughts with me along these lines because I tried to listen and be understanding of her feelings as she was processing her dad's passing. Because she was so young when her dad died, each year as she matures, she sees this processing in a different light. And we go on from there . . . because all Rick's loved ones are in the same boat. To me it's exciting because as we learn we grow. The spiritual knowledge we gain from a departed soul's experience is up to us individually.

Chapter Thirty-Six

A s I come to the closing chapter of this book, my thoughts are on the accumulated knowledge that I have acquired. I feel like I have gone to school and have graduated from the first level, because the continuing levels of learning can go as high as I want them to go. I am speaking in a spiritual sense, though we are also maturing physically along the way. Aging has helped me—because as I've gotten older I'm calmer. This has helped me to listen and be more patient, though I believe I will be working on patience till the day I "kick the bucket"!

As I reflect on the passage of time since Rick has been gone, I have come to the realization that this truly has been a *challenging spiritual experience* for me. From the first moment that I heard of Rick's disappearance, I have never ceased praying, which in turn

> gave me hope and comfort,
> increased my faith,
> kept my sanity intact,
> drew me and my loved ones closer together,
> helped me to be more humble and appreciate everything and everybody around me, and

become more aware of the opportunity of helping others either in a

physical or compassionate sense,

and be more forgiving and patient with others.

I have a peace in my heart now that I did not have before.

When I add all this up it appears that the above listed have been for my betterment. *Sooooo—* is this what is meant by the saying "Good things come out of bad things that happen to us"? I thought of this very thing when Rick left us, but it was not a bit consoling. I was in such a shocking void that nothing anybody said was really consoling. That takes an easing of time.

In conclusion, I realize I became closer to my Creator, just like a very close friend that I could *totally* trust. Through more intense communication, I literally poured out my heart to Him. This in turn gave me the strength and perseverance that I needed. This is how I survived and will continue to survive, because though there will be times of joy in my life, there will also be times of sadness. This is life.

As I worked on completing this book I lost another beloved sibling in my family. It brought all the emotions up again. Just as with Rick—the sick feeling, the frustration and panic, the sorrow. But the experience was not as severe. Perhaps I will save that for another book because it's really a whole story on its own.

I believe that one day what happened to Rick will all come out. Someone will eventually come forward with information, because everyone has a conscience, and as time goes by they will want to lift that guilt from their shoulders. If this never occurs, I'm okay with that, because I've already forgiven anyone who may have been involved in Rick's disappearance. I did this for my own well-being and soul growth.

I was touched when I recently read the following on a sympathy card:

> *Each soul is a beautiful flower that passes from this earth,*
>
> *Only to bloom again in heaven's garden*

That's how I feel about Rick.

When I first started this book, I said that I wanted to jump from point A to point B in time to avoid so much suffering. Well, point B is here now and I survived it okay. Life is truly a mystery and I have experienced that personally. When I get to the "other side," all the answers will be revealed and it will *then* all make sense.

This is my story and I'm sticking to it!

End of story . . . or is it?

Epilogue

On the afternoon of August 28, 2014, Captain Andy Greenstreet, from the Alaska State Troopers came to my door to deliver the following letter:

Dear Mr. & Mrs. Hills:

I begin this letter knowing full well that mere words on a page cannot adequately express the magnitude of apology which you and your family are due based upon errors made by the Alaska State Troopers. A failure on our part has created a circumstance which will undoubtedly bring you and your family a great deal of sorrow during the grieving process and leave you with more questions than answers.

The Alaska State Troopers take great pride in the way we conduct ourselves and the treatment we provide to the residents of our great state. In this instance, I believe that in 2007 we failed to properly communicate valuable information with the State Medical Examiner's Office and ultimately with you.

In September of 2005, approximately one and one-half years after the reported disappearance of your son, the father of another man who had not been seen for several months, found human remains, near where his son has been living. Those remains were obtained by the Alaska State Troopers and sent to the State Medical Examiner's Office to assist in determining identity. In March of 2006 the State Medical Examiner's Office believed identification has been established to the best of their ability and orchestrated release of the remains to the family who had found them.

DNA samples from the remains along with samples from the family were then submitted for comparative purposes to an out of state laboratory. In November of 2007 the laboratory reported the DNA samples were not a match to the family who had found the remains. This information was provided to the Alaska State Troopers and placed into a missing person file. This information was not shared with the State Medical Examiner's Office or with you as we believe it should have been.

This error was not realized until this year, when human remains were discovered near the same area, near Sterling, Alaska, prompting a review of the missing person files.

Additional testing was undertaken in an effort to solidify, with as much accuracy as possible, which set of remains related to which case and ultimately belonged to which family. From this we have learned that the remains provided to the family in 2006, were actually those of your son. This comparative match has been confirmed by familial

DNA testing involving labs in both California and Texas.

The family who was mistakenly provided the remains of your son will be receiving notification concurrent to our meeting with you.

Unfortunately the remains of your son were cremated in accordance with their wishes and were dispersed on the west side of Summit Lake on the Kenai Peninsula. I realize this might not have been the manner you may have elected for end of life arrangements for your son.

I offer my heartfelt apology to you in regards to the way we failed to properly file and disseminate information in this matter. I am hopeful that you can place trust in the Alaska State Troopers in our renewed efforts to resolve this circumstance.

With all of this said, I understand there is nothing I can say that can ever repair the devastation that your family is experiencing. For this, I am truly sorry.

Sincerely,
(His handwritten signature)

Colonel James Cockrell
Director, Alaska State Troopers

Fortunately, we were able to retrieve Rick's remains which were buried above Summit Lake. Later, we had a memorial service at the Catholic Church. Our need for full closure prompted us to have only immediate family in attendance. Afterwards we met with close friends and other family members at Centennial Park on the Kenai River where Rick used to take his kids fishing. It was there where Rick's ashes were dispersed.

All these recent shocking events, of course, were very difficult for us to process. My heart went out to my grandchildren. Tom said that after all this occurred he finally understood what "closure" was about.

And so Reader....my spiritual journey goes on.... I feel that as time goes by this story will continue to develop. There are still too many unanswered questions.

A MOTHER'S TEARS FOR A MISSING SON
A Challenging Spiritual Experience